THE URBAN DESIGN HANDBOOK

Techniques and Working Methods

THE URBAN DESIGN HANDBOOK

Techniques and Working Methods

URBAN DESIGN ASSOCIATES

AUTHORS

Ray Gindroz
principal author

Donald K. Carter
Paul Ostergaard
Rob Robinson
Barry J. Long, Jr.

with contributions by
Donald Kaliszewski
James H. Morgan
David R. Csont
Gregory A. Weimerskirch
Donald Zeilman

PREFACE BY
David Lewis

EDITOR AND
CONTRIBUTING WRITER
Karen Levine

W. W. Norton & Company
New York • London

For information about permission to reproduce selections
from this book, write to Permissions, W. W. Norton &
Company, Inc., 500 Fifth Avenue, New York, NY 10110

The text of this book is composed in Adobe Caslon and
Univers with the display set in Orator.

Book design: WOLFE | DESIGN

Manufacturing by Courier Kendallville, Inc.

Production manager: Leeann Graham

Library of Congress Cataloging-in-Publication Data

The urban design handbook : techniques and working
methods / Urban Design Associates ; authors, Ray
Gindroz, principal author ... [et al.] ; with contributions
by Donald Kaliszewski ... [et al.] ; preface by David
Lewis, editor and contributing writer Karen Levine.
        p. cm.
    Includes index.
    ISBN 0-393-73106-5 (pbk.)
    1. City planning—United States—Methodology.
I. Gindroz, Ray. II. Levine, Karen. III. Urban Design
Associates.

NA9105 .U73 2003
711'.4—dc21   2002026449

W. W. Norton & Company, Inc., 500 Fifth Avenue,
New York, N.Y. 10110
www. wwnorton.com

W. W. Norton & Company Ltd., Castle House,
75/76 Wells Street, LondonW1T 3QT

0 9 8 7 6 5 4 3

PERMISSIONS
The authors gratefully acknowledge permission from
the following sources to reprint material in their control:
Jim Anderson, Anderson Illustration Associates, pages
88, 89, 103, 106, 119, 120, 121, and 128.
Congress for the New Urbanism for the Charter of the
New Urbanism. New York: McGraw-Hill, 1999.
Paul Rocheleau, pages 13 and 41.

CONTENTS

ACKNOWLEDGMENTS

Urban Design Associates would
like to acknowledge the clients whose
projects appear in this book.

BAXTER, SOUTH CAROLINA
Baxter Clear Springs, Inc. and
Celebration Associates

CINCINNATI, OHIO
Hamilton County, The City of Cincinnati
Riverfront Advisors Commission

CLEVELAND, OHIO
University Circle Incorporated

FOREST PARK SOUTHEAST
ST. LOUIS, MISSOURI
McCormack Baron & Associates,
Forest Park Southeast Housing Corporation,
Washington University Medical Center
Revitalization Corporation

GREENVILLE, PENNSYLVANIA
Thiel College

HUNTSVILLE, ALABAMA
The Ledges of Huntsville Mountain

KIMBERLY PARK
WINSTON-SALEM,
NORTH CAROLINA
Housing Authority of the
City of Winston-Salem,
The Harkin Group, L.L.C.

LEXINGTON, KENTUCKY
Bluegrass Tomorrow

LOUISVILLE, KENTUCKY
The City of Louisville and the
Housing Authority of Louisville

MADDEN WELLS
CHICAGO, ILLINOIS
McCormack Baron & Associates and the
City of Chicago Housing Authority

NORFOLK, VIRGINIA
City of Norfolk and the Redevelopment and
Housing Authority of the City of Norfolk,
Tidewater Community College

RIVERSIDE COUNTY, CALIFORNIA
Liberty, The Town Group

STELLA WRIGHT
NEWARK, NEW JERSEY
The Housing Authority of Newark

WESTBURY
PORTSMOUTH, VIRGINIA
The Redevelopment and Housing Authority
of Portsmouth and Cornerstone Development

WHEELER CREEK
WASHINGTON, D.C.
The District of Columbia Housing Authority,
Enterprise Homes,
A and R Development,
Valley Green Skytower Tenant Organization

Over time, Urban Design Associates has developed techniques and working methods for practicing urban design that have proven to be successful for our clients and have distinguished us as a firm. While each project is unique and presents new challenges, certain fundamentals have demonstrated sustained value over time. Paradoxically, by standardizing our techniques and procedures, we have been able to respond more effectively to the individual qualities of each project and place.

This handbook presents those methodologies as a "menu" of tools and techniques. It was first compiled in 1998 as part of the training we provide for new members of UDA. This became especially important as we expanded our intern training program. Each of our urban design teams includes both a first-year and a second-year intern who are most often recent graduates of architecture schools. With a steady influx of new talent into the teams, we saw the need to provide tools that would enable them to quickly become effective in all aspects of an urban design practice.

The working method we describe is one of "uncovery," an approach that helps us understand the impact of physical design on the health and stability of a community. We return, often, to built projects to assess what has worked—and what has not. We use that information in an ongoing way to renew our design principles for buildings, streets, neighborhoods, districts, cities, and regions. For that reason, this document is not just a reference manual, it is also a work in progress.

We were surprised—and gratified—by the level of interest this "in-house" handbook has generated, not only among our fellow professionals, but also among public agencies, developers, and schools of architecture and urban design. Therefore, we decided to make it available to a larger audience.

Although this handbook is designed for our specific practice and group of clients, we believe that many of the techniques and methods will be useful to others. To help the reader in making this transition, we begin with a foreword from our founder, David Lewis, on the firm's origins, followed by a description of UDA and of our projects and client types. Then, in the succeeding chapters, we offer up our techniques and procedures for creating urban designs, pattern books, and architectural design in the hope that you will find them useful in your own pursuit of urban design, whatever your niche in the field may be. Interspersed throughout the book you will find "blue pages" that contain anecdotes, quotes, and design principles we have found to be useful. They appear in the book as they often do in the course of our working sessions—unexpectedly. We have also included a few "war stories" and quotes from various current or former members of UDA whose witty and often wise observations have continued to resonate as the years go by.

Whether you are a newcomer to the profession or an "old hand," we invite you to become familiar with the handbook's content and to refer to it frequently as your basic manual for methodology, techniques, and drawing standards.

RAY GINDROZ, *Principal*
Urban Design Associates

UDA began in the attic of a house on Wallingford Street in the Oakland neighborhood of Pittsburgh in February 1964. We were all pretty young then.

The civil rights movement was gathering momentum. Segregation was a huge issue. Segregated schools, segregated buses, segregated lunch counters, segregated bathrooms.

The Supreme Court ruled that public education had to be integrated. Pittsburgh was one of the targeted cities. Pittsburgh—a city of hills, valleys, and neighborhoods. How, in such a configuration, do you integrate its schools?

In response to this question, we suggested: Ask the citizens. Talk to the parents. Ask what kind of American city they would like their children to grow up in.

Funded by the Education Facilities Lab, a branch of the Ford Foundation, a small group of us began one of the earliest citizen participation processes; and we called ourselves Urban Design Associates because we felt that every person who took part was an associate in urban design.

Our work led us to seeing schools, particularly high schools, not as institutions, but as parts of the city. Schools had libraries, food services, recreation, workshops, and many other facilities that overlapped with already existing public amenities. So why couldn't we de-institutionalize schools and infuse the idea of education as citizen-and-society–building?

It wasn't long before we saw architecture not as the design of separate buildings but as components in the perpetual rebirth of cities.

By the mid- to late sixties, we were convinced that cities are the richest and most complex of all human self-expressions. They are always changing, always evolving, and they are the only art form on which every citizen works.

This realization also convinced us that, at least for ourselves, the traditional role of architects—as the designers of individual "one-off" buildings—needed to be rethought.

We began to see architecture as the physical language of city-and-community–building. We saw the city as a living organism — with a past, which we called "contextual history," and a future in which new buildings acted as the threads that could weave the city's living traditions into new and whole cloth.

How could such an agenda be achieved? The answer was, and is, through urban design.

In the late sixties, urban design was not as widely understood as it is today. But in the late sixties, the inner-city neighborhoods of several American cities erupted into flames and mayhem as the lid flew off decades of suppression and frustration.

Parallel with these events, other important currents were flowing too. One of these was the women's movement. Another — which grew out of the bicentennial — was a sense of urban history and, with it, a renewed pride of place. Yet another, also in the late sixties, was an initiative called Regional / Urban Design Assistant Teams (R / UDATs) by the American Institute of Architects, which put interdisciplinary teams of experts in the service of communities. These were vital and passionate threads in the urban design cloth.

As a result, the participatory processes of urban design, as well as the design recommendations that had public consensus built into them, began to be more widely understood, community by community, city by city.

At the core of what we were doing was a sense of urban design as a language of democracy, a way of linking the individual and the family to the city — house, porch, and street, neighborhood, city.

All of these concerns are eloquent in our work in every dimension — from the scale and detail of a house on a neighborhood street to the scale and complexity of metropolitan form.

Needless to say, all of us can be proud, not only of the work we have done, but of the work you will do, as urban designers continue the quest for more livable cities.

DAVID LEWIS, *Founder*
Urban Design Associates

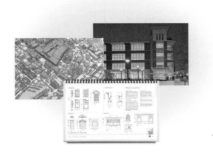

The Firm

Urban Design Associates is a firm composed of architects who design cities, towns, and neighborhoods. Our goal is to create beautiful places with lasting value for the communities they serve.

Design is the creative focus of our process — a participatory process in which we bring together citizens, economists, engineers, architects, developers, policy makers, government officials, and builders to construct humane and appropriate visions for the future.

Our designs build on the unique character and positive qualities inherent in each place in which we are privileged to work. By working at many scales, we find ways of coordinating the design of individual buildings — the public spaces they help create; the neighborhoods, towns, and cities of which they are a part; and the regional culture they celebrate — into a vibrant, viable, and vital urban tapestry. We see that as the mission of urban designers.

Following is an overview of the services we provide, the types of projects in which we are most often engaged, and the clients we serve. While every firm and every project has its own unique character, the concepts presented in this book should have broad applicability to those engaged in urban design, regardless of their specific niche or role in the process.

UDA Pattern Book™ is a ● *trademark of Urban Design Associates.*

DESIGN SERVICES

UDA offers a wide range of design services within three primary categories: urban design; pattern books and design guidelines; and architecture. Because a key component of our role is to create three-dimensional visions for the future, we typically provide services from all three categories on every project we do.

Urban Design. Urban design projects are generally the most public ones. Typically, they entail the creation of master plans, strategic plans, detailed site plans, or visions. The process will almost always engage a large number of people and include sessions open to the general public. Most urban design projects include one main charrette, preceded by a reconnaissance trip, and followed by a series of meetings. The projects typically last anywhere from four to twelve months, although we have some contracts that continue for much longer periods —one for as long as fifteen years!

The essence of our urban design services is the three-dimensional designs UDA prepares in participatory processes with our clients, their various constituencies, and other concerned parties. Regardless of the specific form they take, these designs serve as the vision that guides public policy and investment strategies for each individual project. The tangible products include plans, perspective drawings, models, and detailed drawings of key elements, particularly in the design of public space. These are the visual manifestations of the firm's design recommendations, and they may be published in illustrated reports, memoranda, handbooks, posters, videos, and exhibits.

Pattern Books and Design Guidelines. Once a plan or vision has been created, the next step is to develop the tools that assist with implementation. These tools may take the form of design codes, design guidelines, or pattern books. UDA has found pattern books to be extremely effective in creating neighborhoods. The process engages builders, developers, architects, and real estate professionals in a more technical process. Pattern books enable all participants to understand, embrace, and build from a shared perception of the desired outcomes. The same principles and sequence of events that are used for urban design projects are also used to conduct pattern book projects.

UDA Pattern Books™ are modeled after those used by builders in the past to establish the basic form of buildings and to provide key architectural elements and details. For residential neighborhoods, these may be quite detailed; more general guidelines are used in commercial and downtown development.

Architecture. Similarly, most of our architecture projects are part of implementing an urban design project and thus entail gathering insights and garnering support from a broad-based constituency. When an architecture project is not part of an urban design, we still utilize our process but on a reduced scale, usually with only one major charrette to establish the basic concept and image for the building. Once those are set, the majority of the work consists of the technical implementation.

In order to establish the character of a new development, UDA creates the design image for key buildings within its scope. Our products include conceptual and schematic designs for a wide range of building types including civic or landmark buildings, mixed-use structures, and prototype houses. Construction-oriented phases of the work are done in collaboration with local firms.

MAJOR PROJECT TYPES

UDA applies its urban design philosophy, creative vision, technical expertise, and practical know-how to four major types of projects:

Traditional Mixed-Income Neighborhoods. UDA has a long history of projects that have produced attractive, cohesive, and economically successful traditional mixed-income neighborhoods in highly challenging urban environments. Our work on these types of projects typically consists of:

→   Strategies for existing neighborhoods as part of neighborhood-wide revitalization. This often entails "patching and stitching" declining inner-city neighborhoods with a combination of new construction and restoration.

THE BEGINNING

The year was 1964. UDA's first office was located at 4728 Wallingford Street, in the Oakland section of Pittsburgh. David Lewis founded the firm with a group of Carnegie Mellon graduate students, one of whom was Ray Gindroz. David has ever since proclaimed that he and Ray "co-founded" UDA. The first client was the Ford Foundation.

→   Designs for new neighborhoods in existing cities and towns

→   The transformation of public housing projects into stable, mixed-income neighborhoods

Downtowns, Waterfronts, and Special Districts. The firm is frequently engaged to create visions for developing specific districts within a city, weaving these new districts into the traditional form of the city to attract investment, development, and people. Our work on projects of this type has included:

→   Strategic plans for accommodating and interrelating new development in existing districts

→   Site location studies for specific uses such as a new stadium, arena, shopping center, highway, transit, or convention center

→   Design of key public spaces and the buildings that create them

New Villages and Towns. UDA also designs new developments in rural areas or at the edge of metropolitan areas. These new developments are conceived as traditional towns with carefully designed systems of public open space to preserve natural resources.

Visions. Because our design approach is holistic and multidisciplined, UDA is often involved in developing large-scale visions for metropolitan areas and regions. We produce three-dimensional studies that explore specific issues, such as plans for parks and boulevards, empowerment zone planning, and heritage parks and trails. These visions inherently serve as both the focus for the creative efforts of a wide range of professionals on the project and the spark for other related projects in the area.

WAR STORY NO. I

Make sure the charrette kit is well-stocked. You never know when you'll need extra drafting tape.

ROB ROBINSON
PAUL OSTERGAARD

CLIENTS

Our clients tend to be individuals and organizations that can bring together and coordinate diverse constituencies within a given urban environment to provide essential input to the urban design process. Our clients are typically from:

The Public Sector. Cities and Towns; Redevelopment and Housing Authorities; Local Authorities; County, State, and Federal Agencies

The Private Sector. Residential and Commercial Developers; Master Developers; Corporate Land Holders; Sports Teams; Entertainment Companies; Family Estates; and Financial Agencies

Institutions. Universities; Colleges; Churches; and Institutional Corporations

Not-for-Profit Organizations. Community Development Corporations; Public–Private Partnerships; Foundations; Heritage and Historic Preservation Organizations; Downtown Partnerships; and Business Improvement Districts

ACCENTUATE THE POSITIVE.

ELIMINATE THE NEGATIVE.

DO MESS WITH MR. IN-BETWEEN.

OUR DESIGN APPROACH

IS SIMPLE:

1   Find the best things about a place,
then protect them and build on them.

2   Find the worst problems and design
ways of making them better.

3   Make sure to use the new things to
connect the best things in ways that
fulfill the dreams of the people
we serve.

I

Principles for Urban Design

Urban design is city-building. It brings together the many different parts and pieces of an environment to create a place. At its core is design — an inventive process that draws upon the techniques of many different disciplines to create beautiful, felicitous environments. Therefore, urban designers must be generalists capable of bringing together diverse specialists and technicians to create a unified vision.

Because urban design incorporates so many different disciplines, firms practicing it vary in their core competency. Like Urban Design Associates, some are architectural firms; others are landscape architects, civil engineers, or planners. Each of those different backgrounds and specialties influences the scope of services provided by the respective firms. More and more frequently, firms specializing in urban design are being composed of teams of architects, landscape architects, engineers, and planners.

Whatever the firm's composition in terms of professional discipline(s), the underlying tenets we espouse in this book can be adapted and applied. Our work as a firm of architects practicing urban design embraces a wide range of elements — from the details of individual buildings to the design of entire regions. We focus on the creation of urban space in three dimensions, with a full understanding of the role that the architectural form and the details of buildings and streetscapes play in creating and reflecting the values of diverse, viable, economically successful, human-scale, and ecologically respectful communities.

Since the firm's founding in 1964, UDA has worked diligently to develop and continuously refine a set of urban design principles and methodologies that form the foundation of our professional practice. We believe that our urban design and planning work is successful because it is developed with an understanding of architecture and built form, and that the architecture itself is more successful because it is responsive to urban design and planning issues.

UDA's urban design principles and methodologies have evolved over several decades, and include:

→ Design in a broad-based public process.

→ Create neighborhoods diverse in use and population.

→ Build communities designed for the pedestrian and transit as well as the car.

→ Design cities and towns shaped by physically defined and universally accessible public spaces and community institutions.

→ Create urban places framed by architecture and landscape design that celebrate local history, climate, ecology, and building practice.

PRINCIPLES OF THE NEW URBANISM

We are pleased to note, however, that our approach is in harmony with the Charter of the New Urbanism articulated by the Congress for the New Urbanism in 1996. The Charter is a useful codification of 27 principles that represent the philosophical essence of urban design as we have long practiced it. These principles are at once timely and timeless.

We believe that these fundamental principles form a basis for communication among those engaged in urban design and that we — that is, all of us who are engaged in city-building — need to adhere to them if we are to be successful in creating sustainable communities.

Urban design firms should keep these 27 principles firmly in mind and work collaboratively with clients and stakeholders to restore or create urban centers and towns within coherent metropolitan regions, to reconfigure sprawling suburbs into communities of real neighborhoods and diverse districts, to conserve natural environments, and to preserve our built legacy.

CHARTER OF THE NEW URBANISM

The Congress for the New Urbanism views disinvestment in central cities, the spread of placeless sprawl, increasing separation by race and income, environmental deterioration, loss of agricultural lands and wilderness, and the erosion of society's built heritage as one interrelated community-building challenge.

We stand for the restoration of existing urban centers and towns within coherent metropolitan regions, the reconfiguration of sprawling suburbs into communities of real neighborhoods and diverse districts, the conservation of natural environments, and the preservation of our built legacy.

We recognize that physical solutions by themselves will not solve social and economic problems, but neither can economic vitality, community stability, and environmental health be sustained without a coherent and supportive physical framework.

We advocate the restructuring of public policy and development practices to support the following principles: neighborhoods should be diverse in use and population; communities should be designed for the pedestrian and transit as well as the car; cities and towns should be shaped by physically defined and universally accessible public spaces and community institutions; urban places should be framed by architecture and landscape design that celebrate local history, climate, ecology, and building practice.

We represent a broad-based citizenry, composed of public and private sector leaders, community activists, and multidisciplinary professionals. We are committed to re-establishing the relationship between the art of building and the making of community, through citizen-based participatory planning and design.

We dedicate ourselves to reclaiming our homes, blocks, streets, parks, neighborhoods, districts, towns, cities, regions, and environment.

We assert the following principles to guide public policy, development practice, urban planning, and design.

Charter of the New Urbanism *presents the 27 principles of the New Urbanism, as described by the Congress for the New Urbanism.*

Background: *Signatures of the original signers of the Charter*

Congress for the New Urbanism. *Charter of the New Urbanism.* New York: McGraw-Hill, 1999.

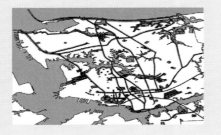

THE REGION: METROPOLIS, CITY, AND TOWN

One

The metropolitan region is a fundamental economic unit of the contemporary world. Governmental cooperation, public policy, physical planning, and economic strategies must reflect this new reality.

Two

Metropolitan regions are finite places with geographic boundaries derived from topography, watersheds, coastlines, farmlands, regional parks, and river basins. The metropolis is made of multiple centers that are cities, towns, and villages, each with its own identifiable center and edges.

Three

The metropolis has a necessary and fragile relationship to its agrarian hinterland and natural landscapes. The relationship is environmental, economic, and cultural. Farmland and nature are as important to the metropolis as the garden is to the house.

Four

Development patterns should not blur or eradicate the edges of the metropolis. Infill development within existing urban areas conserves environmental resources, economic investment, and social fabric, while reclaiming marginal and abandoned areas. Metropolitan regions should develop strategies to encourage such infill development over peripheral expansion.

Five

Where appropriate, new development contiguous to urban boundaries should be organized as neighborhoods and districts, and be integrated with the existing urban pattern. Noncontiguous development should be organized as towns and villages with their own urban edges, and planned for a jobs/housing balance, not as bedroom suburbs.

Six

The development and redevelopment of towns and cities should respect historical patterns, precedents, and boundaries.

Seven

Cities and towns should bring into proximity a broad spectrum of public and private uses to support a regional economy that benefits people of all incomes. Affordable housing should be distributed throughout the region to match job opportunities and to avoid concentrations of poverty.

Eight

The physical organization of the region should be supported by a framework of transportation alternatives. Transit, pedestrian, and bicycle systems should maximize access and mobility throughout the region while reducing dependence upon the automobile.

Nine

Revenues and resources can be shared more cooperatively among the municipalities and centers within regions to avoid destructive competition for tax base and to promote rational coordination of transportation, recreation, public services, housing, and community institutions.

NEIGHBORHOOD, DISTRICT, AND CORRIDOR

Ten

The neighborhood, the district, and the corridor are the essential elements of development and redevelopment in the metropolis. They form identifiable areas that encourage citizens to take responsibility for their maintenance and evolution.

Eleven

Neighborhoods should be compact, pedestrian-friendly, and mixed-use. Districts generally emphasize a special single use, and should follow the principles of neighborhood design when possible. Corridors are regional connectors of neighborhoods and districts; they range from boulevards and rail lines to rivers and parkways.

Twelve

Many activities of daily living should occur within walking distance, allowing independence to those who do not drive, especially the elderly and the young. Interconnected networks of streets should be designed to encourage walking, reduce the number and length of automobile trips, and conserve energy.

Thirteen

Within neighborhoods, a broad range of housing types and price levels can bring people of diverse ages, races, and incomes into daily interaction, strengthening the personal and civic bonds essential to an authentic community.

Fourteen

Transit corridors, when properly planned and coordinated, can help organize metropolitan structure and revitalize urban centers. In contrast, highway corridors should not displace investment from existing centers.

Fifteen

Appropriate building densities and land uses should be within walking distance of transit stops, permitting public transit to become a viable alternative to the automobile.

Sixteen

Concentrations of civic, institutional, and commercial activity should be embedded in neighborhoods and districts, not isolated in remote, single-use complexes. Schools should be sized and located to enable children to walk or bicycle to them.

Seventeen

The economic health and harmonious evolution of neighborhoods, districts, and corridors can be improved through graphic urban design codes that serve as predictable guides for change.

Eighteen

A range of parks, from tot lots and village greens to ballfields and community gardens, should be distributed within neighborhoods. Conservation areas and open lands should be used to define and connect different neighborhoods and districts.

BLOCK, STREET, AND BUILDING

Nineteen

A primary task of all urban architecture and landscape design is the physical definition of streets and public spaces as places of shared use.

Twenty

Individual architectural projects should be seamlessly linked to their surroundings. This issue transcends style.

Twenty one

The revitalization of urban places depends on safety and security. The design of streets and buildings should reinforce safe environments, but not at the expense of accessibility and openness.

Twenty two

In the contemporary metropolis, development must adequately accommodate automobiles. It should do so in ways that respect the pedestrian and the form of public space.

Twenty three

Streets and squares should be safe, comfortable, and interesting to the pedestrian. Properly configured, they encourage walking and enable neighbors to know each other and to protect their communities.

Twenty four

Architecture and landscape design should grow from local climate, topography, history, and building practice.

Twenty five

Civic buildings and public gathering places require important sites to reinforce community identity and the culture of democracy. They deserve distinctive form, because their role is different from that of other buildings and places that constitute the fabric of the city.

Twenty six

All buildings should provide their inhabitants with a clear sense of location, weather, and time. Natural methods of heating and cooling can be more resource-efficient than mechanical systems.

Twenty seven

Preservation and renewal of historic buildings, districts, and landscapes affirm the continuity and evolution of urban society.

In a lecture at the CNU/Harvard debates, historian Robert Fishman compared New Urbanists to a character from one of Jorge Luis Borges' fables.

LABYRINTHS

In "Pierre Menard, Author of the *Quixote*," we meet a 20th-century writer whose life goal is to write (not rewrite or copy) Cervantes' famous book. After much time and labor, he produces a few pages. Astonishingly, they are exactly the same as Cervantes', but, as Borges points out, completely different — because of the context in which they were written. "…Truth, whose mother is history, rival of time, depository of deeds, witness of the past, exemplar and advisor to the present, and the future's counselor" was a truism in Cervantes' time. But it is an astonishing, even radical, statement in the 21st century. From this point of view, truth does not define history as an inquiry into reality, but as its origin. Historical truth is not what happened, but what we judge to have happened.

So, when the New Urbanists revive traditional patterns, that is a radical act — because it runs counter to the formless urban patterns of the last fifty years. It is not replicating, it is re-inventing.

At UDA, we believe the same to be true with architecture as we reconnect it to a long tradition and thus find a key part of how to move forward. We seek out the best in local precedents and incorporate those characteristic elements into the fabric of the new, linking past and future to create harmony across the continuum of space and time.

PROJECT-SPECIFIC DESIGN PRINCIPLES

As strongly as we hold our core principles for urban design and apply them to every project, we also assert that there can be no "cookie cutter" solutions in good urban design. Of necessity, every urban design solution must be unique because each responds to the particular circumstances inherent in the project.

For that reason, in addition to the foundation provided by adhering to core urban design principles, those who practice urban design need to work collaboratively with clients and all stakeholder groups to develop project-specific design principles that evolve from a combination of community-defined needs and aspirations and natural and manmade frameworks. (More will be said about these frameworks in Chapter 2.) In creating and applying these project-specific principles, UDA regularly refers back to our core principles to ensure that the design ideas put forth remain faithful to those larger intentions.

To illustrate what we mean by project-specific design principles, we offer a look at those that UDA developed for the Cincinnati Riverfront. These eight project-specific design principles became the basis for political, financial, and design decisions made by that community.

CINCINNATI RIVERFRONT

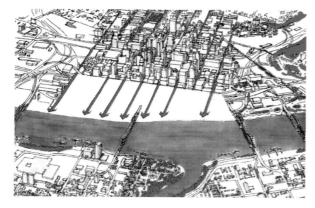

1 Extend the streets and activity of Downtown to the riverfront.

2 Extend Riverfront Park inland to Downtown.

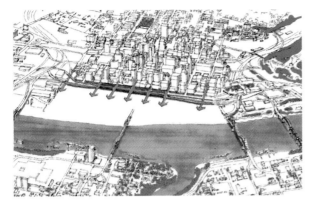

3 Overcome the barrier of
Fort Washington Way Expressway.

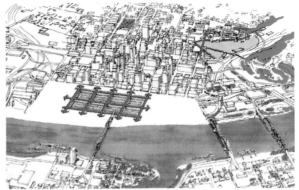

4 Provide parking for the riverfront that serves
Downtown, the stadium, and new development.

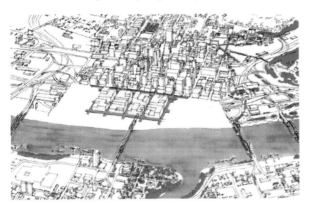

5 Create a series of flexible development sites on
properly scaled new city blocks.

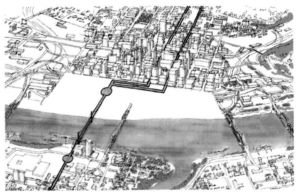

6 Encourage and accommodate transit.

7 Create regional attractions in the
form of a district.

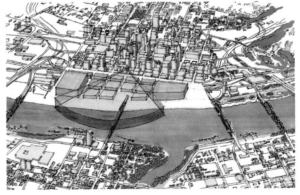

8 Locate large-scale (stadium) structures at
the district's edge to preserve view corridors.

The development of design principles can often facilitate consensus in highly polarized political situations. This proved to be the case in Cincinnati. Voters had approved the construction of two new stadiums—a football and a baseball stadium. Both teams wanted the same central site adjacent to a historic suspension bridge designed by John Roebling. The urban design process prior to the charrette had clearly indicated that Cincinnati citizenry thought that a new riverfront mixed-use district and riverfront park connecting downtown to the waterfront were higher-priority, more appropriate uses for that central site. This clear mandate from the public was reinforced during the charrette, providing Cincinnati's mayor, Roxanne Qualls, and project leadership with access to a neutral public process to guide decision-making on the siting of the two new stadiums. The process—and not politicking or big money wheeling and dealing— led to the most beneficial solution for the city as a whole: development of a new district book-ended by the new stadiums.

The final plan embodies all eight principles.

Urban Structure: Frameworks and Development Patterns

From the form of a region to the detail of a gutter on a cornice, every development area can be viewed from a range of scales. Effective urban design addresses each project by attending to the various scales of design and intervention that are germane to that project, as well as the relationship of the scales to one another.

Scale should be looked at on the following levels:

1 Regional

2 Village, Town, and City

3 Districts and Downtowns

4 Neighborhoods

5 Blocks and Lots

6 Individual Buildings

Collectively, these serve as a "kit of parts," one scale fitting within the other, for practicing urban design. This is a relatively new way of thinking, breaking cities into their pieces and parts so that designers and their clients can see how urban elements are assembled from the standpoint of distinct developmental issues such as natural features, street grids, settlement patterns, building coverage, public space, open space, the integration or isolation of neighborhoods vis-à-vis their surroundings, and so forth.

You'll note that this approach is strongly related to the 27 principles that make up the Charter of the New Urbanism. In our experience, this approach has proven to be highly successful in creating environments that are responsive to the needs of their constituents, that build community, promote a sense of place, and foster personal and civic pride.

Each scale is complex in and of itself; when interrelated with the other scales, the complexity magnifies. To cope with this effectively, we recommend an approach that examines the *framework* and *development patterns* (and the *elements* within each) at the level of detail pertinent to each scale. As we'll cover in more detail in subsequent chapters, we create drawings that document the existing framework and development patterns as well as drawings that visualize the proposed design solutions at each scale pertinent to the project in question.

FRAMEWORKS

To use the human body as an analogy, frameworks are the skeletal structures on which an urban area is constructed. Frameworks can be natural or manmade. Unlike the skeleton of a living being, urban frameworks comprise a mixture of those that are visible and those that exist but have been covered over by development. Either way, frameworks form the armature for community development. Therefore, it is important to understand what the frameworks are for each project you undertake and how they affect the design and development of that particular area.

Natural frameworks consist of the topography of an area, its waterways and undisturbed natural features. Manmade frameworks consist of such features as roads, bridges, rail lines, sewer systems, utilities, and other significant human alterations to the natural landscape, such as designed-in open space, that define the area's shape and overall form.

WAR STORY NO. 2

Always know where you've placed your coffee.

ROB ROBINSON

Frameworks provide access to an urban area and amenities for development. At the largest scales, frameworks provide the basis for building hamlets, villages, towns, and cities. At the smaller scale — that is, within cities and towns — they are the parks and street networks of a neighborhood or district.

DEVELOPMENT PATTERNS

If the frameworks are understood to be the skeleton, then development patterns are the flesh of an urban community. An analysis of the development patterns shows us what, within a well-defined set of categories, has been constructed on a particular framework at a particular scale. Thus, development pattern drawings illustrate both the type and density of use within an area. Historic patterns — even those that may have disappeared through cycles of development and/or decline — should be examined for the clues they provide to valuable local traditions.

At the regional scale, for example, development pattern drawings will depict the hamlets, villages, towns, and cities within the region with their edges clearly defined. At the village, town, and city scale, development patterns identify districts, corridors, and neighborhoods. As you focus down from broad to increasingly more localized scales, the development pattern drawings also become tighter in focus. For example, when you reach the "Blocks and Lots" level, you are looking at elements such as public and private zones, parcels, and access. And, at the individual building level, you are examining community patterns and unique or prevailing architectural styles.

The drawings that follow illustrate how the dual concepts of framework and development patterns can be depicted at each of the six scales.

Regional

1 **Frameworks**
Vision for Bluegrass
Region of Kentucky
Depicts natural elements,
patterns of open space,
major expressways,
road systems, rail and
transit lines, and water
control systems

2 **Development Patterns**
Vision for Bluegrass
Region of Kentucky
Depicts hamlets, villages,
towns, and cities with
their edges clearly defined

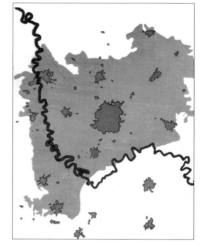

1 Frameworks

2 Development Patterns

Village, Town, and City

1 **Frameworks**
Norfolk, Virginia
Depicts hierarchy of express-
ways, boulevards, and streets;
natural systems and public
open space network; transit;
and utilities

2 **Development Patterns**
Norfolk, Virginia
Depicts neighborhoods.
Other studies indicate
districts and corridors.

2 Development Patterns

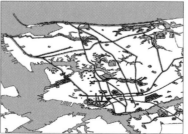

1 Frameworks

Districts and Downtowns

2 Development Patterns

1 Frameworks

1 Frameworks
Downtown Norfolk
On separate drawings, the hierarchy of boulevards and streets, natural systems, and public open space are illustrated to describe an interconnected network of streets and pedestrian space.

2 Development Patterns
Downtown Norfolk
Depicts neighborhoods and districts, building and land use, and key new developments

Neighborhoods

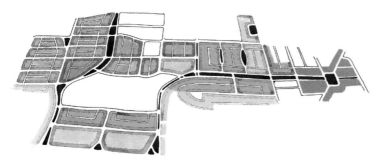

1 Frameworks

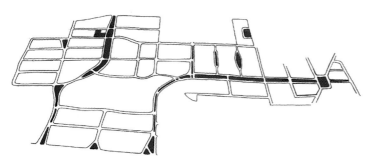

2 Development (Block) Patterns

1 Frameworks
Park DuValle
Louisville, Kentucky
Depicts pattern of streets and public open space

2 Development Patterns
Park DuValle
Louisville, Kentucky
The diagram indicates the block-by-block residential and commercial development of the neighborhood.

Blocks and Lots

1 **Frameworks**

2 **Development Patterns**

Individual Buildings

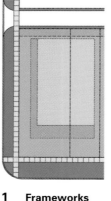

1 **Frameworks**

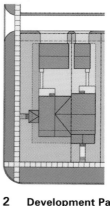

2 **Development Patterns**

Now that you have a better understanding of the overall conceptual approach to tackling urban design projects, we will walk you step-by-step through the urban design process. We begin with how to design the design process.

THE URBAN ASSEMBLY KIT

Our analyses of traditional neighborhoods and cities have helped us to develop a method of thinking about the design of neighborhoods. For example, Ghent, a neighborhood in Norfolk, is a complex structure with many neighborhood streets, each with its own character, a seemingly endless variety of houses with no two exactly alike, and a series of grand and elegant public spaces.

Complex though it is, Ghent, like all American neighborhoods, was built in a short period of time in a remarkably systematic way. Understand that the neighborhood consists of a series of elements, each under control of different entities, but coordinated by the way they are put together.

We think of these elements as an "Urban Assembly Kit" that can be applied to strengthening the fabric of existing neighborhoods or to the creation of new ones. Understanding the separate parts of the neighborhood enables you to both design it and implement it. Through analysis of the individual elements, you gain a full appreciation of the interrelationships among them as well as a foundation for addressing the specified goals in appropriate, achievable ways based on the needs and concerns of the different implementers.

WAR STORY NO. 3

The bag that doesn't make it on the flight will always be the one with the drawings and the slides.

ROBERT FREEDMAN

THE ELEMENTS:
FRAMEWORKS OF STREETS, PUBLIC OPEN SPACE, BLOCKS, LOTS, AND BUILDINGS

Let's take an overall look at the elements that make up our Urban Assembly Kit: a framework of streets, public open space, blocks, lots, and buildings.

The most general element is the framework of streets and public open spaces. The overall hierarchy of streets and parks can be seen clearly when illustrated in the form of a diagrammatic perspective drawing. Institutions and civic buildings find their place (with dignity) in the public open spaces. For example, in Ghent, the art museum is placed at one end of the canal-like space called the Hague. A botanical garden is at the other end of the canal—and a series of churches occupy spaces along its length. Schools are in the middle, in public spaces.

Within this larger framework, blocks of housing and individual streets are placed. A hierarchy exists from house to street to block to neighborhood. While the character, shape, and size of these parts vary with each local condition and in response to local culture, the elements as elements are constants across the nation. It is that commonality of generic form and function that makes UDA's Urban Assembly Kit a valuable tool for city-building.

The revitalization plan for the Park DuValle neighborhood in Louisville, Kentucky, provides an example of how this urban assembly kit is applied. The diagram on the next page illustrates how this relatively simple set of parts is assembled. The result is an urban environment as complex and rich as the traditional neighborhoods from which it gains its inspiration.

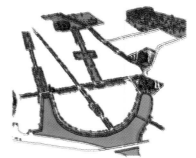

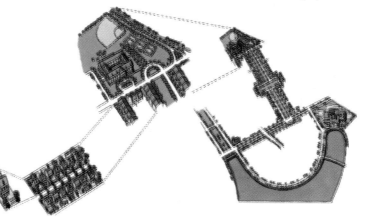

Ghent: framework of streets, public open space, blocks, lots, and buildings

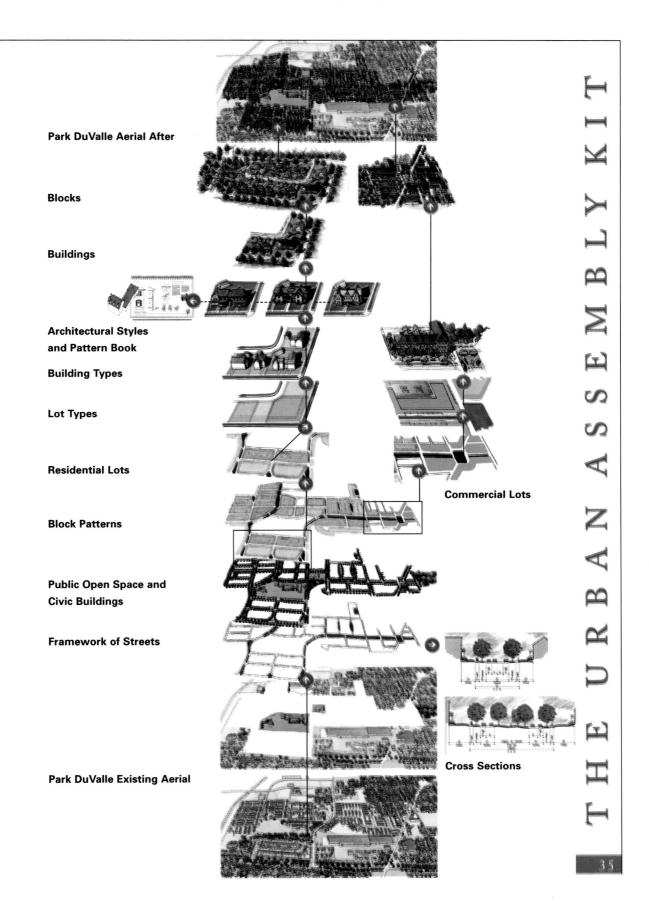

Park DuValle Aerial After

Blocks

Buildings

Architectural Styles
and Pattern Book

Building Types

Lot Types

Residential Lots

Commercial Lots

Block Patterns

Public Open Space and
Civic Buildings

Framework of Streets

Cross Sections

Park DuValle Existing Aerial

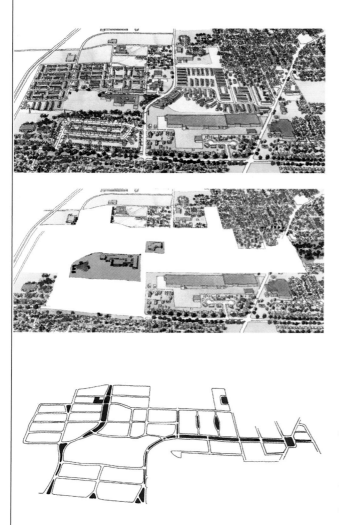

Park DuValle Existing Aerial

An aerial view of the Park DuValle neighborhood as it existed prior to redevelopment shows two isolated public housing projects that were severely cut off from the adjacent neighborhoods. The housing projects were rife with the poverty, crime, and drug trafficking that so often occurs under these circumstances, and the problems were spilling over into the surrounding neighborhoods. Viewed from this perspective, it became clear that part of the solution was to end the isolation of this neighborhood both physically and socioeconomically. The plan, therefore, called for demolishing these public housing structures and creating a new, mixed-income neighborhood that would be linked seamlessly with its adjacent neighborhoods.

Framework of Streets

The first step was to establish the framework of streets. The new interconnected network of streets extends through all parts of the new development and connects them to adjacent neighborhoods. The geometry of the street plan was influenced by Frederick Law Olmsted, whose historic work can be found in so many street and parkscapes in neighborhoods throughout Louisville, including one at the edge of the site. A range of different street patterns exists — from small-scale neighborhood streets with a 28'-0" cartway, to 36'-0" wide community-scale streets, to gracious parkways with landscaped parks separating the two-lane streets.

Cross Sections

A full inventory of public space can be achieved with only six or seven different cross sections. But this inventory must have elements that are relevant and correct for the specific town. Therefore, the proposals needed to be based on research of local models, and then described as a set of standards—here, a wide parkway; there, a small-scale street. For Park DuValle, we measured many of the most beloved streets and spaces in Louisville, which became the model for the different types of street proposed in the plan.

By basing the design on local precedents, it becomes easier to get these elements approved, even by a technocratic process that normally advocates streets that are too big to be human.

Public Open Space and Civic Buildings

This framework is then augmented by public open space and institutions—parks, playing fields, and greens that provide dignified settings for civic buildings such as schools, churches, and other public buildings. This interconnected network of streets and public open space establishes the character and scale of the neighborhood. In Park DuValle, the land was primarily publicly owned and therefore administered by various public agencies. Being able to see the area as a three-dimensional framework facilitated the process by which these agencies collaborated to turn the plan for Park DuValle into reality.

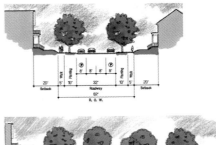

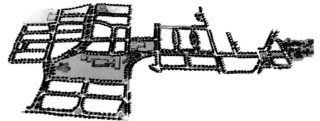

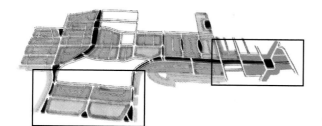

Block Patterns

The framework of streets and open space establishes the addresses for development sites. The streets define blocks for development; blocks are targeted for particular types of development—such as residential or commercial. Within those general categories, other distinctions exist: for example, some blocks may have alleys, others may be serviced from the street. Appropriate dimensions for blocks are also identified. Each block has its own specific criteria.

At Park DuValle, for example, we included commercial blocks, mixed-use blocks, alley-loaded residential blocks, front-loaded residential blocks, and single-sided blocks.

Commercial Blocks

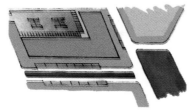

Commercial blocks tend to be larger in order to accommodate the footprints of larger buildings and to provide adequate service and parking behind the buildings. In successful traditional urbanism, parking is available both in front and in the rear of buildings.

Commercial Buildings

In Park DuValle's town center, there is a mix of buildings, some single-use and some with residential over retail.

Residential Blocks

Typically, residential block sizes vary depending on the type of development they carry. In addition, block sizes should be compatible with the existing patterns in the community. At Park DuValle, residential block sizes range from 200'-0" x 300'-0" to 250'-0" x 500'-0". The block designs include provisions, such as setbacks for buildings, to further define the character of the public spaces.

Lot Types

In our Urban Assembly Kit, residential blocks are divided into individual lots. Each block type may have six or seven different lot types. Each lot type might have any one of a number of setback or massing provisions. These provide for variety while preserving the overall aesthetic integrity of the block and the neighborhood. The illustration shows four of the options developed for Park DuValle.

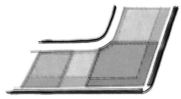

Building Types

Each lot type can accommodate any one of several building types. For example, one illustration for Park DuValle depicts a small apartment building on the corner lot. However, that lot could, alternatively, be used to accommodate a two-unit corner building or a large, single-family house. The illustration also shows how duplexes and single-family houses might be deployed on a single block to help give a mixed-income character to the neighborhood.

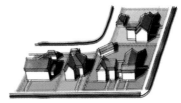

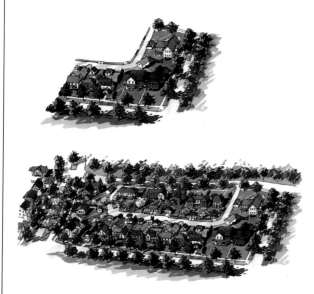

Architectural Style

Architectural style is another important element in the kit. Drawing on the finest characteristics of regional architectural styles and traditions ensures that the new or revitalized neighborhood can claim a place of "belonging" in its larger context. For Park DuValle, this meant creating three architectural styles for each building type. For example, the small apartment building on the corner lot that was mentioned previously was illustrated in three distinct styles: Louisville Classical, Victorian, and Arts & Crafts.

Block Aerial

This assembly kit of simple elements has the power and flexibility to produce a rich and complex environment. The potential for different combinations is practically limitless. Consider Park DuValle. We have three architectural styles for seven building types on seven different lot types, for seven block types that are defined by seven distinct types of street space. The block aerial view only begins to show the incredible breadth of possibilities within the design parameters established for Park DuValle. But it is a testament to the ultimate functionality of the Urban Assembly Kit that it serves as a kit of parts that can be assembled in various ways to respond to local conditions.

Overall Aerial

When all this relatively simple set of parts is assembled, the result is an urban environment as complex and rich as the traditional neighborhoods from which it gains its inspiration. Eleven hundred units of distressed public housing have been replaced by this new mixed-income neighborhood.

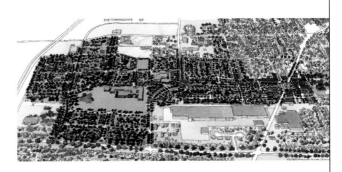

Photo

The "houses" in this photo are, in fact, rental units with a mix of one-third public housing, one-third moderate subsidy, and one-third market rate. Their character is reassuringly Louisville. Their diversity—and the complexity of the neighborhood character—makes these differences invisible and contributes to the overall strength and cohesiveness of the neighborhood.

MEASURING THE URBAN ASSEMBLY KIT

Our Urban Assembly Kit provides a conceptual tool for designing neighborhoods quickly and efficiently in response to the complex dynamics of the process, bringing together community concerns, political issues, and cost and financial constraints, all led by the design.

The framework of streets and open space creates a series of development blocks — the streets are located in part on standard workable sizes for development blocks. The blocks can accommodate a range of possible lot sizes. On each lot size, it is possible to accommodate a number of different building types.

The most permanent and important elements to set early in a process are the frameworks of streets and open space, and the blocks. In any process, and across the span of a project's implementation, there can be many changes to the program, e.g., the type and number of buildings (or units). Therefore, our method enables us to set the overall framework of a plan and still provide flexibility for changing conditions.

However, it is essential to be able to quickly test the capacity of these frameworks of streets and blocks to evaluate whether they meet the program and for cost benefit of the system.

Therefore, we have developed the following method:

1   Draw the framework of streets.

2   Indicate alleys or driveway system.

3   Measure street frontage of lots (front only, i.e., corner lots contribute only one street side to this count) by block and by total plan.

4   Develop prototype lot and building types, e.g., 40'-0" wide single-family lots, 25'-0" wide townhouse lots, 55'-0" wide duplex lots, 70'-0" wide 6 flat lots, etc.

5   Establish alternative mixes of unit types, e.g., 40% single-family; 20% townhouse, 30% duplex, and 10% apartments.

6 Use the spreadsheet below by inserting the number of units in each type. The spreadsheet will then indicate the number of lineal feet of frontage required for the total of each unit type and for the mix.

An alternative method is to calculate the net density of various combinations of lot type within a block. For example, one block type might be 12 units to the acre (single-family and duplex) while another might be 30 units per acre (mostly apartments and townhouses).

Urban Assembly Kit:
Determining the Housing Mix and the Capacity of the Plan

Building unit type	Lot type	Avg. lineal feet of frontage/ building unit	No. of households/ building unit	Lineal feet of frontage/ housing unit	Assumed housing unit mix	Resulting no. of households	Resulting no. of buildings	Resulting building mix	Total lineal feet required
Single-family	on cottage lot	40	1	40	40%	211	211	61.54%	8448
Single-family	on neighbhd. lot	60	1	60	5%	26	26	7.69%	1584
Duplex	on neighbhd. lot	60	2	30	20%	106	53	15.38%	3168
Triplex	on estate lot	70	3	23	20%	106	35	10.26%	2464
4-unit apt.	on estate lot	80	4	20	5%	26	7	1.92%	528
4-unit apt.	on common lot	100	4	40	5%	26	7	1.92%	660
6-unit apt.	on common lot	100	6	17	5%	26	4	1.28%	440
					100%	527	343	100%	17292

Required no. of housing units   528

Required net acreage assuming 100' lot depth   39.70
Assumed net to gross efficiency of plan   0.65
Required gross acreage   65.50

Total lineal feet/no. of bldg. units   50.38
Total lineal feet/housing unit   32.75

MAKE SURE THE PROCESS IS HONEST AND THAT EVERYONE WHO HAS A ROLE HAS A VOICE. THEN LET THE PROCESS LEAD DECISIONS AND DESIGNS.

Designing the Process

It may sound strange to say, but the first step in the process—and the most important task for every project—is to design the design process itself. Sometimes you make a first attempt at designing the design process as part of the proposal to a potential client. Most often, however, you meet at the beginning of a project with the client's leadership group, collaborating with them to craft a process that will actively engage a broad range of individuals and constituencies.

Where do you start?

PROJECTS DETERMINE THE PROCESS

The design of the process must respond to the circumstances under which the project will be conducted and the role it will play in the life of the community. For urban design work, there are many such roles. Here are a few examples:

Forming Treaties

Urban design efforts are often born in conflict. The urban design document can serve as a treaty to bring about a truce among warring parties. The design process has a role in establishing that truce. Thus, the process must be structured to enable each side to feel that it has been heard adequately. Urban Design Associates often employs a combination of individual meetings with each faction and public meetings in which all factions participate to facilitate a truce. By focusing on the issues, presenting thoughtful analyses, and urging people to come forward with both their concerns and their ideas, the design process can bring people together to solve problems in a nonconfrontational way.

For example, in a project UDA undertook to redesign a public housing project in Philadelphia, over 300 people from all walks of life gathered in a church hall to discuss the problems of the area, express their hopes for the future, and react to some preliminary design proposals. Years of conflict between residents of the project, the adjacent working-class neighborhood, the nearby affluent community, and a business district had left many people feeling hostile and isolated. At the end of the meeting, a tattooed young man who had lived in the neighborhood next to the public housing project said, "The plan is already working. I have lived all my life without ever setting foot in the project or talking with someone who lived there. I found myself sitting next to a woman from the project and agreed with some of her ideas. I was surprised that she had a sense of humor and was someone I really liked as a person. The process is bringing people together."

Forging Visions

Urban designers are often asked to provide a vision for communities that will enable them to attract investment and coordinate the efforts of many disparate and even discordant interests. By providing such a vision, it is possible to bring individual efforts together to create a whole that is greater than the sum of its parts.

Such a process must reach out and engage all of the constituencies so that their interests are seriously considered and accommodated in the Vision. For this reason, vision-building is a very public process that seeks to cultivate widespread support for the Vision. We often refer to this type of process as "building a bandwagon." Success is measured by how crowded it gets.

Devising Strategies

When you are asked, as we most often are, to develop a strategic plan, rather than a comprehensive plan, your best course of action is to focus the process on short-term initiatives—yet you must always keep both a comprehensive view of the context and an appreciation for future possibilities in mind.

Participants in these projects consist not only of those who are stakeholders in the specific project under consideration, but also those who are concerned with the success of the overall form of the area and its citizens. For example, Norfolk's Downtown planning process included several individual initiatives within the overall planning efforts. While a Downtown Committee provided oversight, separate task forces (such as those for the Tidewater Community College project) were formed to guide the work.

Creating Good Locations

Many projects begin their lives with sites that are deteriorated or simply thought of as not good locations. Yet clients have ambitions for these sites, enthusiastic ideas for what they can become through focused effort. That means that a key part of the job is to create a good location, to visualize an achievable new image for the site, one that will attract customers, businesses, home buyers, and investors to that location. The process involves focus groups, market research, and the involvement of those who have a stake in the site. Such processes are sometimes open and public; in other cases, because of property control issues, they may be less public, but strive, nevertheless, to be inclusive.

Marketing Sites or Areas

Transforming public housing projects into mixed-income neighborhoods, reviving downtowns to bring a suburban population flocking to retail and cultural activities, or developing industrial zones that will rely on attracting the right kind of businesses, all require marketing programs. The urban design documents, as well as the publicity around the process, become part of the overall marketing effort. The process begins with gathering input and support, then moves into overt marketing activities once consensus has been achieved on the design. By making the marketing of a site or an area the primary goal of the design process, it is often possible to gain support from a wide range of constituencies, many of whom would never have expected to be on the same team.

Downtown Norfolk
By demolishing half of a 1970s parking structure, Freemason Street was reopened to link the long-vacant properties of the Granby area with the revitalized Freemason District and Waterfront.

Marketing Materials
Portsmouth's invitation-to-builders package provided marketing support for the development of a new mixed-income neighborhood.

Projects often entail a mix of the five types described above. For example, a neighborhood revitalization program may serve as a means of achieving a treaty and creating a good address in deteriorated inner-city neighborhoods. UDA Pattern Books (discussed fully in Chapter 5) often serve as a means of building a bandwagon, of strategically bringing together groups to unite around a central vision or shared set of goals, and of marketing the project. Architecture projects (discussed in Chapter 6) can provide the built result that then stands as a symbol of the process, as well as being the catalyst that starts the implementation process.

CREATING THE STRUCTURE FOR THE PROCESS

Each type and scale of project will likely require a different organizational structure, some simple, others more complex. Whatever structure is selected, there are key questions that must be addressed.

Who's in Charge?

Always remember that urban designers are advisors to the process, not the policy makers or implementers of programs. Therefore, it is essential that a person or organization or group of people be clearly "in charge" and responsible for making decisions. Sometimes this is a governing body, such as a city council, that deliberates in public sessions and is accountable to the public. In other cases, it is a community organization with a less formal structure, or a private developer, or a corporation that must invest its resources and be true to its mission. It may be a foundation with a specific social purpose or an institution with its own leadership and accountability structure.

Without clear leadership, the urban designer may feel somewhat adrift and inadvertently slip into the role of the policy maker — or, at least, be perceived by the public as having become the policy maker. *Avoid this at all costs!* In some such situations, you may elect to withdraw from a project because you believe it can not succeed under the circumstances. A good instinct to have if you want to survive and thrive in urban design is to know when to duck.

The organizational structure, however it is ultimately configured, must enable us as urban designers to bring information, ideas, and concepts to the policy makers in a form they can deal with effectively.

Who Participates in the Process?

Urban design is a collaborative effort that creatively engages all constituents. Recommendations and decisions need to be made at each of the scales of analysis that were presented in Chapter 2. Each of these different scales of design has an impact on the quality of the public realm and on the lives of the people within it. For that reason, it is essential to encourage the many different constituents who claim ownership of the area (and who bear the responsibility for both creating and maintaining it) to actively engage in the urban design process with the urban design team and the client.

The Urban Design Team. UDA is organized into a series of teams of four or five persons each. Teams stay together and work on a group of projects. They have their own filing cabinets, drawing storage areas, charrette equipment, and location in the studio. They are responsible for four to eight projects at any given time. The project manager works with the principals to schedule work for each week, month, and six-month period. Management tasks including billing, distribution of work, and scheduling are done by the project managers.

On each project, the team is augmented by one or more principals, and by specialists including a perspectivist, architectural design advisor, publisher, or process strategist. Most teams are guided by a principal-in-charge whose role varies by the scale and type of the project as well as by professional relationship with the client group. Some variation on this general approach to project teams should work for most firms regardless of size.

Because urban design is so complex, it requires creative dialogue and collaboration among members of the urban design firm as well as with public participants, consultants, and clients. By establishing permanent teams, communication among members is facilitated and methods of working are tailored and improved. Each team develops its own techniques and personality within the general standardized techniques described in this handbook.

UDA Team Member Roles and Responsibilities

UDA has developed specific roles for various team members that help keep the process flowing smoothly. The principal-in-charge is expected to:

→ Attend every client meeting, focus group meeting, and public meeting

→ Participate in the analysis and design working sessions

→ Provide senior direction to the process

The second principal typically:

→ Acts as senior advisor (often, the client group relies upon this individual for overall philosophical or political advice)

→ Provides design leadership both in the studio and on charrettes

→ Contributes specialized skills to areas of the project not covered by other members of the team

The design team leader is responsible for the:

→ Design development

→ Schedule

→ Budget

→ Invoicing

→ Process logistics

→ Production of the interim and final products

The assistant design team leader is responsible for:

→ Assisting the project manager in project management tasks

→ Serving as a designer on the project

Designers (consisting of experienced designers as well as first- and second-year interns) are responsible for:

→ The full range of work items during a project, including preparing base materials, x-rays, design sketches, perspectives, elevations, report layouts, and model studies

→ Managing photographic work including reconnaissance, archiving materials for presentations, and marketing files such as project sheets and slide presentations

The perspectivist is responsible for:

→ Meeting with the team to determine perspective needs as well as to identify the desired views and required base materials

→ Providing perspective bases prior to a charrette

→ Participating in the charrettes so that the drawings are created within the context of the process

Graphics production personnel are responsible for:

→ Formatting documents

→ Maintaining continuity

→ Publishing UDA products (e.g., master plans, pattern books, architectural designs)

→ Cataloguing and archiving electronic materials

Shaker Heights
steering committee

The Client. As we noted in the Introduction, UDA serves a variety of clients. While clients may come from many different quarters, most often urban design clients are public agencies, community groups, or private developers. Although these organizations may have several people actively engaged in the project, it is preferable that the client assign one project manager who will be the primary contact for the design firm's project manager on a day-to-day basis.

The Steering Committee. A steering committee may also have been selected to guide the project. The steering committee's role is to provide an overview of the process and make policy decisions. An optimum size for a steering committee is twelve to fifteen members.

It is crucial that the steering committee be representative of the individuals and interest groups who have a stake in the project. For a neighborhood, this usually includes residents, business people, social service providers, cultural groups, institutions, school officials, elected officials, and government staff (planning, public safety, etc.). For a Downtown Master Plan, the steering committee may be chaired by the mayor of the city with appointed members who represent all of the downtown constituencies, including residents, merchants, bankers, foundations, public agencies, institutions, and some public officials.

In some circumstances, steering committees may find it useful to form subcommittees to consider each district or interest area. Ideas can then emerge and be tested at the subcommittee level and, after review and refinement, be taken first to the steering committee and then on to the city council.

Constituency Representatives. For every project, a broad spectrum of participants should also be included as part of the design process. These individuals should come from a cross section of:

→ Those who know the area best
→ Those who will feel the greatest impact from any changes that might be made
→ Those who are capable of implementing and financing the effort
→ Those who control the political and bureaucratic processes
→ The general public
→ Those who are often disenfranchised: the poor, minorities, and immigrants

As we discuss each of the specific steps in our process (see Chapter 4), you will see that there are opportunities for constituency representatives to have a significant voice in shaping the project. In some cases, the input of broad-based constituencies takes place solely at the early stages of the process and may be limited to the collection of information and clarification of stakeholder needs, preferences, and concerns. In other projects, participation occurs at specifically designated critical points in the process—for instance, at a public design charrette. Then there are the projects where participation is more discretionary and continues throughout the design process.

Participants vary from one project type to another. In neighborhoods, it is the residents who have the most knowledge about their community. They are also the people who will be affected most directly by any action recommended in a plan. Therefore, you must find ways to ensure that they are involved in the process. Without their participation, the likelihood that a plan can succeed is severely diminished. Residents are not, however, the only essential participants, especially in troubled neighborhoods. Direct connections must be established between the residents of a neighborhood and the power structure of the city. We always strive to actively engage political leaders in order to foster this necessary dialogue.

In downtowns, the participants will be different. Here, they are more likely to include a broad spectrum of representatives from the major corporations, retail merchants, cultural attractions, real estate developers and leasing agents, government officials, the city's urban planners (if they are not, in fact, the client), and concerned citizens who have an occupational and/or personal interest in the vitality of their city's downtown district.

Whoever the participants may be — and they are often an intriguing cast of characters — the basic premise to employ is one of inclusion. The aim is to obtain and incorporate as many points of view as possible so that you can create the richest, most responsive designs possible.

How Do You Provide for Broad-based Participation and Input?

There are several methods for encouraging broad-based participation and input: advisory committees, focus groups, individual interviews, and charrettes. Whatever mechanisms you use to obtain broad-based participation and input, the process must also include mechanisms for delivering written records of each encounter. Subsequent meetings should begin with a recap of the previous session to create the sense that you are building on the input provided.

Advisory Committees. In addition to the leadership group, the organizational structure must contain a clearly understood mechanism for broad-based participation among all stakeholders. In some cases, this is best accomplished with one or more advisory committees that provide information to us, review our work, and make recommendations that are then submitted to the leadership group.

It is essential that each participant clearly understand his or her role. For example, if those serving on an advisory committee believe they have the power to make and implement decisions, there can be frustration and anger that can cause the process to unravel and, ultimately, to fail.

Focus Group Meetings and Individual Interviews. Less formal participation can be achieved through focus group meetings and individual interviews. It is the urban design firm's responsibility to record and synthesize this information for the advisory and steering committees.

Charrettes. Charrettes are an integral part of many of the urban design processes. These one- to three-day intense, on-site working sessions bring designers and a wide range of participants together to share, develop, and test ideas. When you as designers sit in the place to be designed, rather than in your own studios, you open the design process to a much wider array of possibilities and influences. When other participants — residents, politicians, developers — sit with you as you sketch, and often start sketching themselves, they see new possibilities for resolving old conflicts and developing new forms.

A project may entail one or more charrettes. We will describe how a charrette is organized and conducted in more detail later.

At this point, the most important thing for you to learn and remember about charrettes is this one cardinal rule:

No matter how many encounters you may have with participants, the first time you meet people, you are asking questions, not giving answers. You do not come with set ideas or solutions. You develop them in response to the understanding you obtain through the process.

How Is the Schedule Established?

Another important parameter that must be determined at the outset of a project is the timing needed to meet the client's objectives. At the beginning of each process, you develop a schedule, a sequence of meetings, and a list of the final work products. The complexity of the choreography of the process and its organizational structure are usually directly proportional to the scope of the project and thus have a direct influence on the schedule you create.

It is essential that all participants understand the timing and work plan in advance so they can arrange their schedules accordingly. People will not participate in a program that has no clear end in sight, and they become frustrated if the process drags on without an understanding of where it is going. Consequently, a clearly articulated and agreed-on schedule with defined progress review points is essential to the success of each of our projects.

Timing Is Everything, So How Long Is Too Long?

Because each step in the urban design process must continue to build consensus and clarity of purpose among a wide range of people and interests, the individual steps cannot last too long. Timing is everything. We have found that shorter is much better than longer. Processes that do not move forward expeditiously fail to build the necessary momentum, and that's damaging — potentially even fatal — to the success of the project.

Consequently, once a consensus is reached, it must be documented and acted upon before new circumstances and changing political dynamics erode it. For that reason, it has been our experience that we can often achieve much more in six to nine months than in two years. In fact, we have had considerable success with processes conducted in as little as two to three months when all of the players are identified and the issues defined up front. Whatever the time frame, the results of a process should be published and circulated as soon as possible in order to keep the bandwagon moving.

The urban design process functions like a camera lens. When you first look, the image is blurry, out of focus. At each step of the process—each turn of the lens, so to speak— the image comes into tighter focus until the ultimate resolution is sharp and a design solution emerges.

The Urban Design Process: Three Phases

No matter how simple or complex a project may be, and regardless of whether the time frame is two months or two years, UDA's urban design process always consists of start-up activities followed by three distinct project phases:

→ **Phase One**:   Understanding—Figuring Out What's Going On

→ **Phase Two**:   Exploring—Trying Out Ideas, Exploring Alternatives

→ **Phase Three**: Deciding What to Do—Developing the Plan

We have found that this approach provides for the widest range of participation, the greatest opportunities for consensus-building, the strongest likelihood of success, and the best possibility for spawning subsequent corollary projects. Application of this phased approach ensures that even the most complex projects can be managed in a clear and systematic process designed to produce the best possible results for our clients.

Each phase consists of numerous steps. The remainder of this chapter is devoted to walking you through each of the steps and describing specifically what it is UDA does at each step, why we do it, and how.

Illustrating the Process: Kimberly Park

To illustrate our process, examples will be drawn primarily from the Kimberly Park project in Winston-Salem, North Carolina. The Kimberly Park project is a master planning effort that focuses on replacing 556 barracks-like public housing units with 475 new homes in a mixed-income neighborhood that will link several traditional Winston-Salem neighborhoods. Architectural features of these new homes will draw upon the respected characteristics of Winston-Salem's architectural styles. The new development will have strong edges that both define it and link it with the adjacent neighborhoods. In addition, the project calls for restoring a natural streambed that had been landfilled, integrating it into a continuous linear park that will establish a new relationship between previously isolated neighborhoods and the opportunities of the city.

UDA's Tools and Techniques

Over the years, UDA has developed a series of tools and techniques that are an integral part of our process for urban design. As we walk you through each step in the process, we will introduce the relevant tools and techniques at the point in the sequence when the need for them typically first arises.

Helpful Hint: For your first reading of this handbook, we recommend that you read the step-by-step information that follows in the order in which it is presented. This will enable you to become familiar with UDA's process by working through it conceptually, in sequence, seeing how each step builds on the previous ones. Then, when you refer back to a specific step or activity in the future, you'll understand how it fits within its broader context and the ramifications that the things you do at any given moment may have on subsequent aspects of a project.

PROJECT START-UP

Each project begins when we receive an invitation to submit a proposal from a client who has identified a need and is searching for a solution. Before preparing a proposal, we have some initial conversations to determine the type of process and category of service(s) required.

As described in the Introduction, UDA's services fall within three primary categories: urban design projects, UDA Pattern Book projects, and architecture projects. Each of the three follows a similar process, but with different emphases.

The balance of Chapter 4 discusses the three phases of our urban design process. Chapter 5 addresses UDA Pattern Books and Chapter 6, architecture projects.

Ideally, a project manager and one or more principals are involved with the marketing coordinator in putting together the proposal. Scheduling the work is usually part of the contract negotiation. Once the contract has been signed, work can commence, beginning with Phase One.

WAR STORY NO. 4

When you ask me to find the image of the street with the houses and the tree in the middle, please be more specific.

MICHELE FICKES

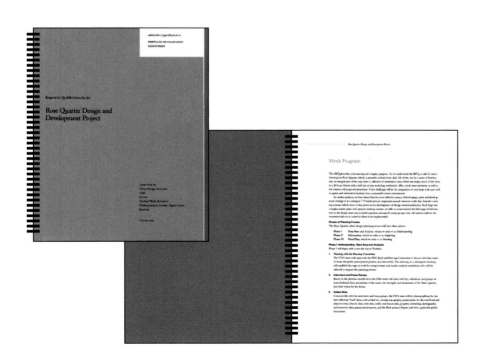

PHASE ONE: UNDERSTANDING

Figuring Out What's Going On

Phase One is all about figuring out what's going on. Until we have done that, we have no basis for doing any meaningful design work. Phase One requires that we synthesize our technical analysis, face-to-face discussions with participants, and hands-on experience of the site to develop a clear understanding of both the physical issues of the design and the perceptions and aspirations of the community and all participants.

Phase One consists of:

→   Pre-Trip Preparation

→   Trip One

    →   Meeting with the Client (and Steering Committee)

    →   Meeting with Focus Groups

    →   Interviews

    →   Public Meeting (optional)

    →   Data-Gathering

→   Analysis of Existing Conditions

Pre-Trip Preparation

After we have received a signed agreement or a letter to proceed, it's time to schedule our first trip. Because the success of this trip sets the tone for the entire process, it is essential that Trip One be exceptionally well-organized and carefully orchestrated. It is better to delay the trip than embark on it without proper arrangements.

The client must be intimately involved in setting up Trip One, including:

→   Organizing a steering committee if one does not exist

→   Arranging for data collection

→   Scheduling all of the formal activities of Trip One (the initial meeting with client representatives and the steering committee, focus group meetings, and the public meeting, if one is to be held during Trip One)

The UDA team also has a number of things to do to prepare for Trip One. Everyone on the team needs to become as familiar as possible with the overall layout and general features of the area in which we will be working *before* the trip. This means we need to gather and acquaint ourselves with:

→ AAA map (Learn the street names before the trip!)

→ U.S. geological survey (USGS) map of the project area

→ All materials gathered during the interview and selection process

→ All materials supplied by the client

This advance preparation enables us to be knowledgeable enough to ask meaningful questions and to understand, in context, the information, goals, and objectives of each of the project's constituencies. There is nothing that instills confidence in a client and their constituents faster than a team that has done its homework. This positive tone and perception, established at the beginning of the process, can prove to be very important as the project progresses.

Trip One

When we, and our client, have finished preparing, it's time for Trip One. This trip usually entails two to three full days and involves the principal-in-charge, the project manager, and the designers. Often, one or more of the subconsultants will join us, especially the market consultant. Depending on flight times and distance, the team often travels the night before so that we can get an early start on Day One.

Meeting with the Client (and Steering Committee). The initial meeting with the client serves as the official kickoff of the project. The meeting should be the first scheduled event on Day One of Trip One and should, whenever possible, include the steering committee, if one has been formed.

The agenda for that initial meeting consists of:

→ Review of the overall planning process, scope of work, and schedule

→ Review of the agenda for Trip One

→ Discussion of the make-up of the focus groups

→ Direction on collecting hard data (zoning, historic, traffic, topographic, etc.)

USGS maps of the project area

To locate base map materials, City Hall planning departments and historical societies are the best places to start. USGS maps are also useful. Aerial photographers may have material you can use.

Meeting with Focus Groups. The focus groups are the key to collecting soft data about the project. Usually there are between four and six focus group meetings held during Trip One, with each meeting lasting between 1½ and 2 hours. We hope to obtain initial input from a broad array of constituents during the focus group sessions; therefore, the groups are typically formed from:

→   Residents

→   City staff (including zoning, public safety, public works, engineering)

→   Business persons

→   Institutions (schools, social service agencies, cultural groups)

→   Historic preservation groups

→   Elected officials (mayor, council, etc.)

Focus group meetings should be scheduled at times convenient for the attendees. This often involves breakfast, lunch, and evening meetings.

At the start of each focus group session, the participants are given a description and schedule of the planning process, the purpose of the plan, and their role in consensus-building. All are then asked these same three questions, and their individual responses are recorded on a flip chart:

1   What do you like best about your neighborhood?
(strengths, good things, assets)

2   What do you like least about your neighborhood?
(weaknesses, bad things, liabilities)

3   What is your vision for the future of your neighborhood?

The last question is designed to invite blue sky dreaming among the participants. It encourages each to imagine his or her ideal version of the neighborhood five or ten years in the future. It invites them to envision it as if it already exists. What does it look like? What is there? Who is there? We ask them to describe places that they have visited — or know of — that are like their vision for their own neighborhood. And we record all of these — every wish, every hope, every dream — for it is from these aspirations that we can begin to form a collective vision.

It is often useful to show a base drawing with the boundaries of the project for orientation and discussion. We also ask what are the best and worst places in the area, and note them on maps using colored dots. During this meeting, our function is to ask questions, not provide answers. Our goal is to promote collaboration. Introducing potential solutions this early in the process tends to shut that participation down, sending people straight into reactive mode. That polarization can be like a pernicious disease to the urban design process.

Interviews. It may be desirable to conduct individual interviews with key leaders in various constituent groups.

Active listening is required if these interviews are to be worthwhile. That means that the individuals doing the questioning must do more than work from a prepared list of questions. They must be skillful enough to probe for levels of meaning in the interviewee's responses, evoking as much depth as possible from each individual interviewed. The ability to read between the lines, perceive an underlying meaning, and elicit more information is essential to producing maximum value from these interviews.

Public Meeting (optional). Sometimes, due to local politics or at the request of the client or steering committee, it is necessary to have a public meeting in addition to the focus groups. We handle the public meeting like a large focus group, first describing why we are all assembled and the process we will use, then asking the same three questions we asked of the focus group participants. If the turnout at the public meeting exceeds 25 people, we introduce ourselves and describe the process, then break into smaller groups to handle the three questions.

Data-Gathering. Data-gathering is a crucial part of Trip One. In addition to the soft data we acquire during the focus groups, there are three other types of information we need to gather during Trip One:

→ Existing hard data

→ Photo reconnaissance

→ Measurements

Best and worst places in the area, as indicated on the above map

WAR STORY NO. 6

Be aware of where you're taking photos.

JONATHAN KLINE

Imagine a van carrying the firm's personnel (and perhaps representative participants also) driving around town, pulling up curbside, people spilling out of all the doors with cameras and tape measures and measuring wheels, taking photos, making sketches, estimating heights, and taking measurements from all different angles. Then, as suddenly as we appeared, we disappear back into the van, driving on to the next place, where this frenetic activity repeats itself.

Existing Hard Data. The existing hard data we need to collect includes:

→   Base maps (land use, buildings, building conditions, roads, topography, zoning, parks and open space, wetlands, hazardous/contaminated sites, etc.)

Base maps are the single most important form of hard data we gather on the first trip. Be resourceful, be a detective. It's important to make the base maps as accurate as possible. We need to compare aerial photographs with the base maps, checking for what's on the ground now in terms of actual usage. Be aware that the maps you collect from other sources are often not up-to-date.

As you gather this data, remember that it is necessary to get input at the appropriate scales to create a regional base map, a city-wide base map, and a neighborhood (or project area) base map.

→   Master plans

→   Zoning ordinances

→   Historic surveys and written histories

→   Market studies, including demographic data, ownership, evaluations, and areas

→   Traffic studies

→   Aerial photos (planimetric and oblique)

→   Others as relevant to the project

WAR STORY NO. 7

Always make sure all team members are fully inside the car before putting it in gear.

STEVE AUTERMAN

Photo Reconnaissance. The goal of photo reconnaissance is to document the conditions at the site as well as the adjacent areas that affect the site. In addition, photos should be taken of other neighborhoods in the city or county that are considered to be exemplary by the client and the steering committee.

If you believe, as we do, that each new act of city-building must respond to the culture and traditions of its town and region, finding examplars is an important component of the data-gathering process. These buildings, public spaces, and environments represent more than just excellent specimens by the standards of the citizens of that place. They also provide historical precedents for consideration during the design process.

Photo reconnaissance should be done in three formats:

→   Color slides

→   Color prints

→   Digital images

Video reconnaissance may be done for some projects. The typical set of images should include:

→   Streets

→   Sidewalks

→   House elevations

→   House details

→   Parks

→   Apartment buildings

→   Schools

→   Others as warranted

Measurements. It is convenient to take measurements at the same time you do your photo reconnaissance. Just as we photograph in precedent neighborhoods as well as at our site, we also measure in all of these locations. Measurements are taken by hand with measuring wheels or tape measures. Experience teaches that accurate measurements are important to *getting it right.*

1 Find the good address.

2 Photograph panorama from the sidewalk.

3 Photograph elevations.

Among the things to measure are:

→ Street widths, curb-to-curb

→ Intersections

→ Right-of-way widths

→ Tree lawn widths

→ Sidewalk widths

→ Cartway widths

→ Front yards

→ Building setbacks

→ Building widths

→ Space between buildings

→ Lot widths

→ Others as pertinent to the site

Analysis of Existing Conditions

At the beginning of the analysis process, the team needs to make some fundamental decisions in order to optimize the efficiency of the process. These considerations include:

→ The scale to be used for base maps

→ Cartoons of potential UDA X-Rays® (diagnostic drawings that show key aspects of existing and proposed future conditions) before the actual drawings are prepared (see page 73 for more information about UDA X-Rays)

→ The scale of UDA X-Rays (we often use three or four different scales: regional, city-wide, impact area, and immediate area)

→ The scale of the model (with thought given to its portability for air travel or overnight delivery service)

→ Selection of the aerial perspective view

→ The potential multiple uses of the base maps and UDA X-Rays for slide presentations and for the final report (The goal is to do them well and do them only once!)

UDA X-Rays® is a trademark of Urban Design Associates.

The analysis done during Phase One is really rather straightforward. While we do not necessarily do all of the following tasks for every project, the list below presents a fairly comprehensive view of what we are likely to do at this stage of the project. Generally speaking, our tasks now are to:

1 Create a list of the base data collected.

2 Send a copy of this list to the client.

3 Label and organize photographs, slides, and digital images.

4 Write a summary of the focus group meetings.

This is intended to be an accurate, balanced, and unbiased summation of the information gathered during the focus groups. It is our role to report the findings, not provide spin on their meaning.

5 Prepare accurate base maps (see examples on pages 69 through 72) showing:

→ The site within its regional context

→ The site within its city-wide context

→ The site within its impact area

→ The site within its immediate area

We view these drawings as a kind of encyclopedia that provides considerable information of different kinds without interpretation. Creating these base maps is neither a simple nor a mechanical process. We construct base maps that show streets as spaces bounded by individual buildings, and these, when taken together with all the other details within the public realm, create a place. Because each element of the city is administered by a separate department, all of this information often has not been aggregated on a set of standardized and/or current base maps.

Our task is one of patiently searching for and compiling the information we require. Finding street maps is usually fairly easy, but rarely do they include the details of sidewalk and planting strips, or correct building configurations, or property lines.

Project name and number

Dearborn 1154
Perferred Plan Perspective
JDA February, 1999

Date

Image name and type

D I D
Y O U
K N O W ?

Baron Haussmann's most difficult and costly task in rebuilding Paris was getting a survey. Some things never change!

Never underestimate the time or ingenuity it will take to gather the source material, or the creative energy you will need to combine the maps at the four scales required to understand the site's relationship to its contexts.

Beware of Geographic Information Systems software (GIS) maps and out-of-date city maps. The most sophisticated computerized base maps are sometimes the least accurate! Sanborn Maps™, often available in the tax offices, have been one of our most reliable sources.

The map preparation process typically requires between 30 and 60 days.

6   Read and summarize key reports and previous studies.

7   Prepare street and site sections.

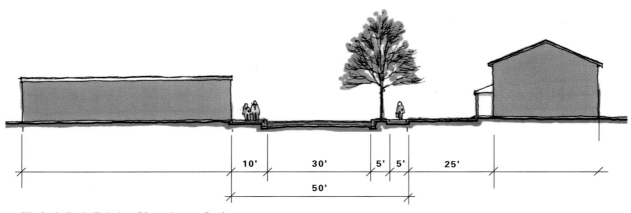

Kimberly Park: Existing Glenn Avenue Section

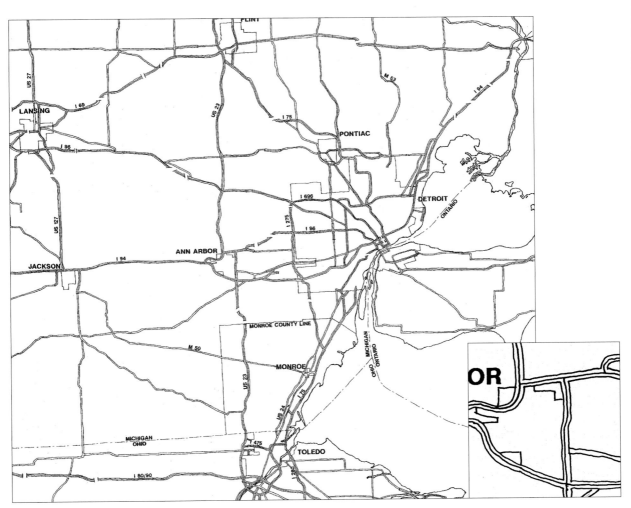

Actual Size:
Please note line weights and line style.

Identifies:
Highways, major natural features, and settlement patterns

Purpose:
Orientation

REGIONAL BASE MAP

SITE WITHIN ITS REGIONAL CONTEXT

Actual Size:
Please note line weights
and line style.

Identifies:
Streets, cartways, landmarks,
institutions, open space,
and major natural features

Purpose:
Provides an understanding of
the overall form of the city
and its impact on the site

CITY-WIDE BASE MAP

SITE WITHIN ITS CITY-WIDE CONTEXT

Typical scale: 1" = 400' to 2000'

Actual Size:
Please note line weights
and line style.

Identifies:
Streets with rights-of-way,
cartways, sidewalks,
buildings, natural features,
and topography

Purpose:
Provides a more detailed
understanding of the physical form of the area that has
a direct impact on the site
and that will experience
the greatest benefit from
the development

IMPACT AREA BASE MAP

SITE WITHIN ITS IMPACT AREA

Typical scale: 1" = 200' to 1000'

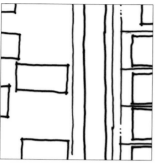

Actual Size:
Please note line weights
and line style.

Identifies:
All buildings, property lines,
streets and sidewalks, and
topography

Purpose:
Provides all information
needed to develop a design
for the site that will ensure
that it becomes an integral
part of the neighborhood

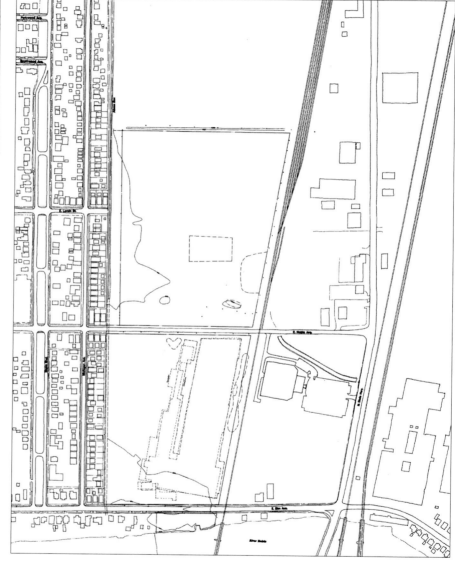

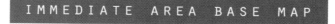

IMMEDIATE AREA BASE MAP

SITE WITHIN ITS IMMEDIATE AREA

Typical scale: 1" = 100' to 400'

8   Prepare UDA X-Ray drawings of existing conditions.

UDA has developed a series of proprietary graphic analyses that we call x-rays. Using the base maps (described previously), we take each category of information and place it on a drawing all by itself. The site is always placed in the middle of the sheet regardless of the size of the area represented in the overall scope of the drawing. How large an area will be covered in each x-ray is determined by the principal-in-charge.

At this stage, we are preparing x-rays of existing conditions. (During Phase Two, we will be developing x-rays depicting proposed future conditions.) The x-rays of existing conditions address each of the different scales of base map. For example, we may create individual x-rays that show highways and arterial roads at the regional scale, expressways and highways at the city-wide scale, and street patterns at the neighborhood scale. Each x-ray, at each scale, provides its own clues to the form of the site and ways in which its future can be influenced by what we do on it.

Although the UDA X-Ray preparation process can be time-consuming and tedious, the first step is a quick sketch, created in a team working session. This will reveal some of the patterns and issues of the project and help identify those x-rays that are most critical. The accuracy and graphic quality of these drawings is important for later slide presentations, board-mounted exhibitions, and the final report.

The most efficient way to produce the x-rays is to complete them as an in-house charrette in a specified, concentrated time period that has a definite deadline. The team should be heavily scheduled to complete the work within that time frame with little or no distraction from other project assignments. Before the x-ray charrette begins, accurate and complete base maps must be prepared, and a set of cartoons must be sketched, reviewed, and revised by the UDA project team.

Regional X-Rays

Settlement patterns

Highways and arterial roads

Open space and natural features

City-Wide X-Rays

(Typical scale: 1" = 400' to 2000')

Residential settlement patterns

Expressways and highways

Street grids

Open space and institutions

Railroad and industrial uses

Commercial land uses

Impact Area X-Rays

(Typical scale: 1" = 200' to 1000')

District drawing

Historic patterns

Street patterns

Topography/natural features

Open space and institutions

Land use portrait

Buildings (figure-ground)

Parcels

Portrait of conditions

Immediate Area X-Rays

(Typical scale: 1" = 100' to 400')

Area drawing

Historic patterns

Street patterns

Topography/natural features

Open space and institutions

Land use portrait

Buildings (figure-ground)

Parcels

Vacant land/buildings

Surface/structured parking

Portrait of conditions

From time to time, we may also prepare sketch x-rays in public working sessions to uncover problems and identify opportunities for improvement. During the course of the design process, the x-rays become more detailed and accurate, refining our understanding of the challenges that need to be addressed in our recommended design solutions.

X-rays are subjective; interpreting them requires experience. Therefore, it is important to have a group review process in-house before presenting these to clients and their constituents.

We have found that our clients value highly our unique UDA X-Ray analysis sequences. A typical set of x-rays for a project might include the list of x-rays at left.

The graphic techniques we have developed for producing UDA X-Rays are key to their success as an analytical tool. On the following pages, you will find the specifications you should follow when preparing UDA X-Rays of existing conditions. These specifications address format, scale, colors, and line weights.

UDA's drawing style for x-rays is neither too detailed nor too loose. The examples that follow on pages 77–87 in this handbook illustrate our recommended drawing style and are accompanied by an explanation of each layer we examine during this phase of our process. The selection of x-rays presented here is from our Kimberly Park project; however, other types of x-rays may be desirable depending on individual project requirements.

The first step is to identify the orientation points at each scale. Typically these include an outline of the site itself as well as a major landmark or two (e.g., a river valley, mountain, significant building, or complex of buildings).

UDA X-Ray examples >

**Drawing is taking
a pencil for a walk
to see what
it encounters
along the way.**

PAUL KLEE

**Standard Specifications
for Existing Conditions
X-Rays and Land Use**

Expressways	Warm Red	
Arterial highways	Orange	
Regional settlement patterns	Pale Orange	
Topography *(lowest elevation to highest)*	Dark Green Bright Green Lime Green	
	Medium Green Light Green Pale Green	
	Yellow Green Lemon Yellow	
Open space systems	Bright Green	
Institutional buildings	Purple	
Commercial buildings	Salmon	
Residential buildings (houses)	Lemon Yellow	
(multi-family)	Dark Yellow	
Parking lots and alleys	Grey Beige	
Industrial buildings	Light Blue	
Vacant lots / buildings	Tones of Grey	
Parks and public open space	Green	
Water	Deep Blue	
Background (if any)	Tan	

Type of X-Ray:
Prototype

Size:
24" x 36" *or* 32" x 40"
depending on the area
covered

**Typical Line Weight
and Style (actual size):**
Actual size details of line
weight and style at left

X-rays should be expres-
sive and communicate
essential form rather
than be mechanical and
precise in detail. At the
regional, city-wide, and
impact area scales, they
should be careful freehand
drawings with line
weights that exaggerate
actual scale in order to
enable the form to be
read well at a distance.
More detailed drawings
such as the building
coverage plans can be
either done as freehand
tracings or as digitally
generated drawings.

Type of X-Ray:

Settlement patterns

View: Plan

Description:

Residential settlement patterns are outlined in general form by tracing over the edges of residential areas as indicated on either a USGS map, aerial photograph, or land use map. Where there are major gaps within such areas, they should be outlined and appear as "holes" in the fabric.

Observation:

The site could be described as either in the center of an "island-like" settlement area, or as connecting two separated areas. There is a large "hole" in the fabric on each side of the site. These qualities indicate a site that is somewhat separate from other neighborhoods.

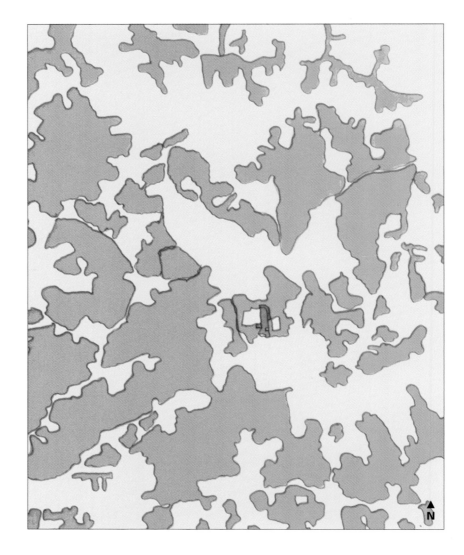

CITY-WIDE

EXISTING CONDITIONS X-RAYS

Typical scale: 1" = 400' to 2000'

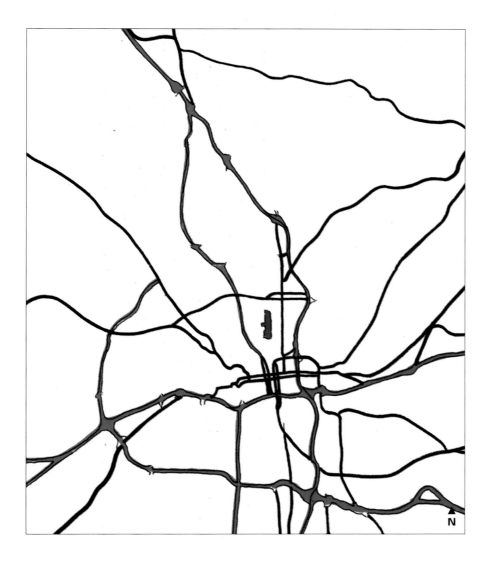

Type of X-Ray:
Highways and arterial roads

View: Plan

Description:
There is a network of highways that is both south and east of the site. The arterial pattern creates an irregular, discontinuous network. The site is in the center of an area bounded by arterial roads and that has a somewhat coherent pattern.

Observation:
The site is near both arterial roads and two highway interchanges, but does not connect directly to them. There are no through roads that touch its boundaries or pass through it.

CITY-WIDE

EXISTING CONDITIONS X-RAYS

Typical scale: 1" = 400' to 2000'

Type of X-Ray:
Streambeds

View: Plan

Description:
Streambeds are indicated in blue, and the sloped land on each side is indicated in green.

Observation:
The continuous patterns of streambeds and their tributaries is a strong form in the landscape. The site straddles one of these. This may help explain the irregular residential settlement and street patterns.

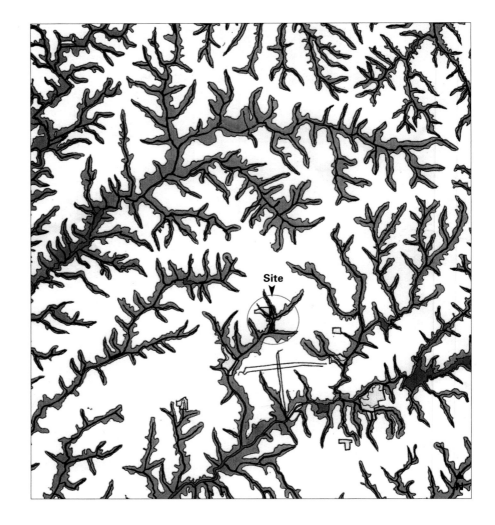

Site

CITY-WIDE

EXISTING CONDITIONS X-RAYS

Typical scale: 1" = 400' to 2000'

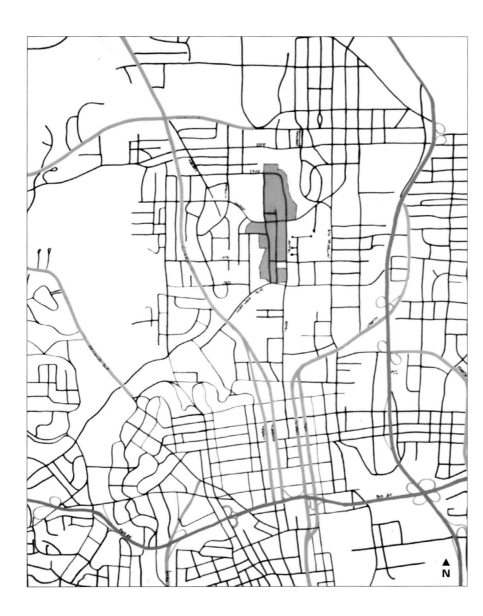

Type of X-Ray:
Street grids

View: Plan

Description:
Three scales of street patterns are indicated: highways, arterials, and local streets. The local street patterns vary in different areas around the site and include curvilinear streets, small-scale inter-connected block patterns, and irregular grids.

Observation:
The site is in the center of the most fragmented grid pattern. It has only one through connection and is not linked to the adjacent areas in any direction. It contrasts with the more regular neighborhood patterns to the south and west.

IMPACT AREA

EXISTING CONDITIONS X-RAYS

Typical scale: 1" = 200' to 1000'

Type of X-Ray:
Building patterns
(figure-ground)

View: Plan

Description:
Building footprints are
rendered in solid black.
They are the "figure" of
the pattern, and the space
between them is the
"ground." Large industrial,
commercial, and institu-
tional buildings are generally
located in the south and
east, and in the areas
indicated on the railroad
and industrial uses x-ray.
Institutional buildings
of a campus are visible on
the upper left. The rest is
a small-scale pattern
of houses.

Observation:
The most continuous and
regular patterns of houses
are in the southwest, north,
and northeast areas of the
drawing. Buildings on the
site are larger and more
regimented in form than
those in the adjacent
traditional neighborhoods,
which further separates
them from each other.

Note: It is often useful on a separate x-ray to examine the historic
patterns of development in addition to the existing conditions.

EXISTING CONDITIONS X-RAYS

Typical scale: 1" = 200' to 1000'

Type of X-Ray:
Railroad and industrial uses

View: Plan

Description:
The railroad lines, indicated in black, create a continuous pattern that runs generally north/south, immediately east of the site with an east/west line south of the site. Because rail lines served industry, there is a continuous pattern of industrial uses along them.

Observation:
These patterns explain some of the gaps in the residential settlement patterns and the way in which the site and its immediate context are isolated from other residential areas.

N

IMPACT AREA

EXISTING CONDITIONS X-RAYS

Typical scale: 1" = 200' to 1000'

Type of X-Ray:
Street patterns

View: Plan

Description:
One large north/south arterial is located in the immediate area. There are two east/west connections that serve the site. The local street pattern is extremely irregular, is discontinuous in the area of the site, and has a variety of different block dimensions.

Observation:
At the larger scale, the site's lack of connection to its adjacent areas is more apparent. With only two direct links to the main road, it is isolated.

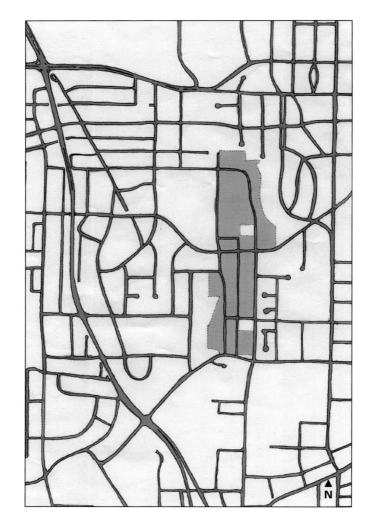

IMMEDIATE AREA

EXISTING CONDITIONS X-RAYS

Typical scale: 1" = 100' to 400'

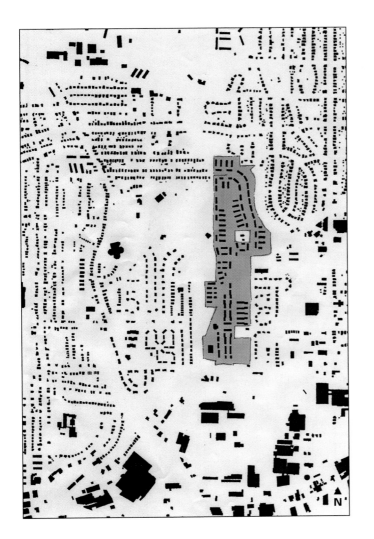

Type of X-Ray:
Building patterns
(figure-ground)

View: Plan

Description:
The site has the most
regular and large repeating
building forms. Adjacent
neighborhoods have smaller
buildings on a variety of
streets, and the large industrial and institutional
buildings are at the edge
of the drawing.

Observation:
At this larger scale, the
contrast between the
institutional-scale housing,
buildings on the site, and
the more personal and small-
scale houses in adjacent
neighborhoods is more stark.
The gaps in fabric are also
more formidable. The degree
of separation between the
"project" and the "neighborhood" is more clear.

Note: It is often useful on a separate x-ray to examine old historic
patterns that pre-date the patterns created by public housing.

IMMEDIATE AREA

EXISTING CONDITIONS X-RAYS

Typical scale: 1" = 100' to 400'

Type of X-Ray:
Topography and natural
features

View: Plan

Description:
This x-ray combines two
types of information. The
topography is indicated with
a range of colors with the
darkest color for the lowest
elevation. The site is indicated with the buildings in
bright red.

Observation:
This illustrates the way in
which the site, which was
filled when developed,
interrupts the natural form
of the streambed.

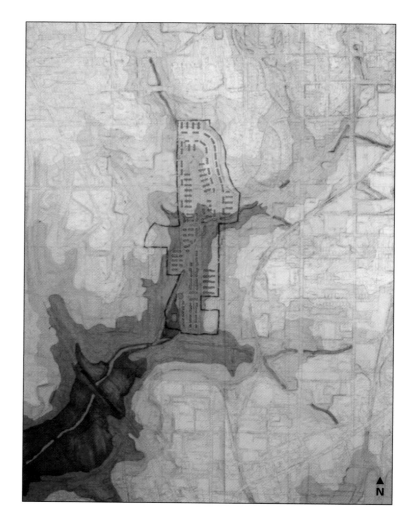

IMMEDIATE AREA

EXISTING CONDITIONS X-RAYS

Typical scale: 1" = 100' to 400'

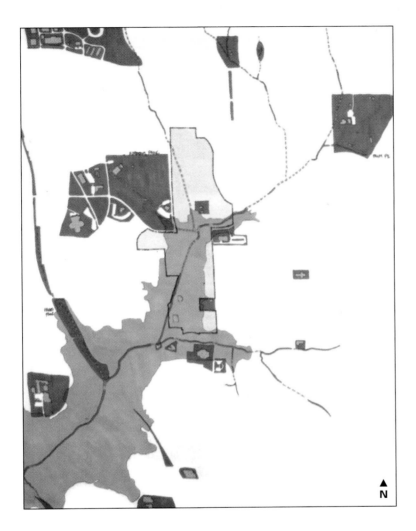

Type of X-Ray:
Open space, natural features, and institutions

View: Plan

Description:
Recreational fields, parks, schools, churches, and other civic uses are indicated, as are the center lines of the streambed in this area.

Observation:
Many institutions and recreation facilities are located near the streambeds.

IMMEDIATE AREA

EXISTING CONDITIONS X-RAYS

Typical scale: 1" = 100' to 400'

9 Prepare existing conditions eye-level perspective drawings.

Often constructed from photos taken during Trip One, these drawings are at eye level, wherever possible, and focus on key aspects of the site that will be addressed during development of the plan.

Type of Drawings:
Existing conditions eye-level perspectives

Description:
The selection of these views is made both during the initial site visit and the charrette. Views are chosen if they represent the problems of the site, which will need to be addressed in the design solutions. They also should cover the variety of conditions and problems that will need to be addressed.

Observation:
The barracks-like uniformity of the buildings and the distance between them conveys a barren, alienated image. The retaining walls and awkward site conditions indicate a poorly conceived and built development.

Type of Drawing:
Existing conditions

View:
Aerial perspective

Description:
The project area is in the center of the drawing, which extends to cover most of the immediate impact area. The adjacent open space, topographic change, and nearby neighborhoods are indicated realistically.

Observation:
The barracks-like form of the public housing project on the site stands in sharp contrast to the more individualized and personal character of the houses in adjacent neighborhoods. The site appears to be on a platform, strangely flat and separated from the rolling landscape. There is no evidence of the streambed and valley, which was such an important landscape feature on the x-rays. It was buried by the development. The drainage culverts that had been put in were failing, and terrible plumbing problems resulted.

10 Prepare an existing conditions aerial perspective.

Typically, we prepare an "existing conditions" aerial perspective of the project area, which serves as another tool to help people visualize the current condition of the project area and its immediate environs. Produced using an oblique photo as reference, this existing conditions aerial perspective helps stimulate discussion during the charrettes that take place during Phase Two. This drawing, in subsequent phases of the project, serves as a base drawing on which design proposals are inserted for testing.

11 Prepare a scale model (not always required).

The scale model is helpful to the analysis because it presents the context in three-dimensional form. In preparing the model, we use layers for topography, wooden or plastic blocks for buildings, and colored plans for natural features and landmarks. Typical scales are 1" = 50' and 1" = 20'.

12 Prepare a summary analysis.

In the summary analysis, we identify the good things and the bad things, the best places and the worst places, within the project area. These guide us in the development of a portrait of the site.

13 Prepare a rendered land use plan for the project area.

A rendered land use plan is an objective representation of the facts—an encyclopedia of all the information about the site gathered on one drawing. Uses for each building are indicated on the drawing through a standardized color palette. This drawing, in subsequent phases of the project, serves as a base drawing on which design proposals are inserted for testing.

14 Prepare a portrait.

The portrait drawing enables us to see the "good" and "bad" things in relationship to one another. Although similar to the rendered land use plan, in the portrait we render the good things in warm, friendly colors and the bad things in dreary grays and browns. Overlays containing special features or some of our preliminary design ideas are rendered with extra-bright colors. This serves as our first draft of a framework within which we can begin to develop design alternatives. We find it essential to develop sketch design concepts on this basis because it forces us to consider the impact of every design idea on its overall context. This drawing, in subsequent phases of the project, serves as a base drawing on which design proposals are inserted for testing.

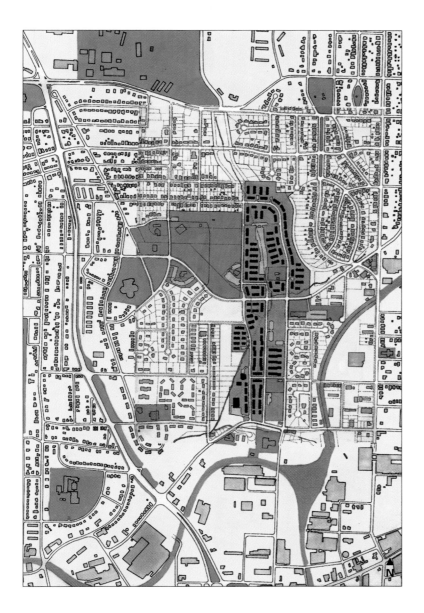

Type of Drawing:

Existing Conditions
Base Plan

View: Plan

Description:

All of the basic information
of the site and its context
are described. Buildings are
indicated and colored to
indicate use. The roads,
streets, parks, open space,
and natural features are
described.

Observation:

The colors are muted so
it can be used as a base
drawing on which to place
design proposals to understand their impact on the
context. This is a reference
document that we often
refer to as the "encyclopedia":
everything is indicated and
therefore no clear patterns
emerge, as they did in
the x-rays.

IMMEDIATE AREA

EXISTING CONDITIONS BASE PLAN

Typical scale: 1" = 100' to 400'

Type of Drawing:
Portrait

View: Plan

Description:

As in the land use plan, many of the elements of the site and its context are indicated. The portrait, however, is not neutral. The positive elements are described in bright, cheery versions of the land use colors, while the negative factors are indicated in dark and dreary colors. Like Oscar Wilde's *Picture of Dorian Gray*, this drawing reveals the problems of the area. Unlike Wilde's portrait, it also reveals the strengths and good qualities. The identification of strengths and weaknesses is a synthesis of the team's analysis and the perceptions and observations of the participants in the process.

Observation:

The site itself and the area around it contain many problems, including deteriorating properties, incompatible uses, and vacant land. The strongest areas are somewhat removed from the site.

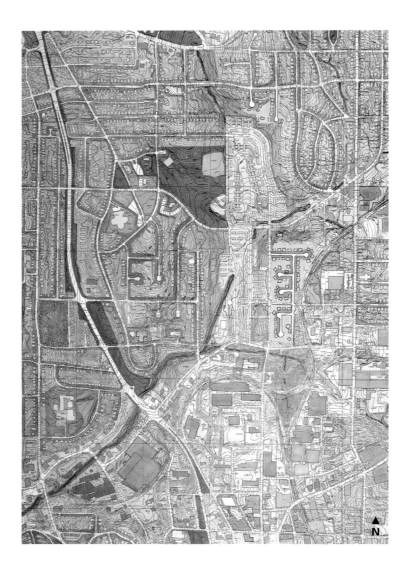

IMMEDIATE AREA

EXISTING CONDITIONS PORTRAIT

Typical scale: 1" = 100' to 400'

Existing Base Plan Colors:

Background buildings	Light Salmon
Background yards/lots	Tan
Good open space	Medium Green
Strong residential	Lemon Yellow
Vacant sites	Light Grey
Vacant buildings	Medium Grey
Institutions and civic buildings	Light Purple

Existing Portrait Colors (Dorian Gray):

also includes above colors

Strong neighborhoods (yards/lots)	Pale Green
Strong commercial	Salmon
Strong multi-family	Dark Yellow
Parking lots/alleys	Grey Beige
Industrial	Light Blue

Proposed Plan Colors:

Green space	Bright Green
Park trees	Medium Green
Street trees	Dark Green
Water	Deep Blue
Front yards	Medium Green
Back yards	Light Green
New single-family residential	Yellow Orange
New multi-family residential	Orange
New office/commercial	Salmon
New retail/mixed-use	Warm Red
New institutional	Purple
Existing institutions	Light Purple
Shadows	Dark Grey

The proposed designs are drawn and boldly colored so that, when placed on the existing base plan, they are clearly delineated.

LISTEN CAREFULLY...

to the words people say

to what is being said between the lines

to what is being said in people's eyes

to what is being said with gestures and body language

PHASE TWO: EXPLORING

Trying Out Ideas, Exploring Alternatives

Phase Two is the part of the process devoted to trying out ideas, investigating options, and exploring alternatives.

Phase Two consists of three parts:

→ Preparing for and conducting a one-day, in-house charrette

→ Preparing for and conducting a three-day, on-site charrette (Trip Two)

→ Documenting the charrette and filing the materials

If the term charrette is new to you, you may find it interesting to know that it means "little cart" in French. The reference is thought to harken back to the 19th-century École des Beaux-Arts in Paris where it is said that proctors circulated at the end of final exams collecting student drawings on little carts. Students, frantic to finish, would jump onto the "charrette," putting the final flourishes on their projects as they rolled toward the deadline. The meaning of "charrette" has evolved over time and has come to refer to the intense brainstorming process that leads to a finished design. While we no longer literally leap onto carts as they roll down the aisles, the charrette process is the key to creating the boisterously enthusiastic and successful bandwagon we mentioned previously in this guide.

Preparing for and Conducting an In-House Charrette

Our in-house charrette is critical to the success of the on-site charrette. The in-house charrette should be scheduled a week or more before the on-site charrette. Ideally, all principals will take part in some portion of the in-house charrette. Our key subconsultants are usually, but not always, included in the in-house charrette. Sometimes, the client participates as well.

Who attends, other than the staff, is a judgment call best made by the principal-in-charge of the project. Generally, budget, timing, and politics are all factors in the decision regarding who participates.

WAR STORY NO. 9

The most important slide in your presentation is usually the one that's overexposed.

DON CARTER

The Expected Outcomes of the In-House Charrette. The in-house charrette is intended to accomplish the following:

→ Review the base map and "portrait" drawings for accuracy, readability, and graphic sharpness.

→ Review and revise the street and site sections.

→ Review, revise, and augment the UDA X-Ray drawings.

→ Review the focus group summaries.

→ Review the photos and slides for completeness, and identify any gaps to be filled.

→ Develop a preliminary series of urban design principles (usually five to ten) that seem to be emerging from the analysis and that will be used to guide the development of design alternatives.

→ Develop preliminary design alternatives to test the urban design principles and to get a feel for the dynamics of the site.

→ Make final adjustments to the traveling charrette team, and develop and/or refine the on-site charrette schedule.

→ Assign the following tasks:

　→ Make final revisions to the base data and analysis drawings.

　→ Take slides of the base drawings, sections, and UDA X-Rays.

　→ Revise the urban design principles.

　→ Prepare the charrette kit.

　→ Make final preparations for the on-site charrette, and coordinate with the client.

The Flow of the In-House Charrette. How do we typically conduct an in-house charrette? First, we array the drawings around the room, then look at them, one by one. We talk about each x-ray. What clues do we find in the pattern of streets on the grids x-ray? What areas seem to have an appropriately scaled, interconnected grid of streets? Which areas are disconnected and fragmented? Where are the blocks short, encouraging interaction among streets and, therefore, fostering a sense of community? Where are they not? How is the neighborhood connected to the rest of the city? How effective is this? What changes have occurred in the street pattern over time? What are people's favorite places? How does the pattern on the drawing relate to that? Where are the worst problems, and is the pattern on the x-ray part of the problem? This questioning continues from x-ray to x-ray.

During this process, we document key points for each x-ray. With so much information, it is easy to get lost in details and tangents. Consequently, we use this charrette to winnow out those x-rays that do not add new information. The ones that contain the most pertinent information are collated and prepared for public presentation and publication.

Once we have settled on a set of drawings, we ask two key questions to guide us in our exploration of alternatives:

1   In view of the goals of this effort, what are the five or six most important positive qualities we have seen in the x-rays?

2   What are the five or six most serious problems to overcome?

These are then distilled into one or two sentences for each x-ray and become part of the preliminary report to the community.

In-House Design Review

Following the in-house charrette — and immediately before the team leaves for the on-site charrette — we hold an in-house design review in which the whole office participates. *The value of this cannot be overstated.* We present work-to-date, and everyone has the opportunity to comment and make suggestions. This gives us the opportunity to try out and "de-bug" our ideas with one another, before we put them center stage in front of our clients and their constituents.

Kimberly Park In-House Charrette

You've reviewed the Kimberly Park x-rays on the previous pages. Now let's look at what we've "uncovered" through that process:

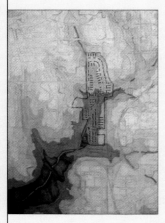

Five most important positive qualities:

1 The rolling topography and continuous pattern of streambeds is a strong form that could tie the parts of the community together.

2 Institutions and open space are located in relationship to these streambeds.

3 There are nearby neighborhoods to which the rebuilt development could relate.

4 The site is not far from arterial roads and streets leading to other neighborhoods.

5 The site is near Downtown and not far from major educational institutions.

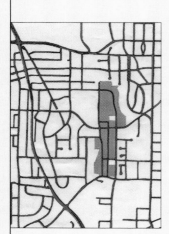

Five most serious problems to overcome:

1 The site is isolated and separated from both other neighborhoods and the amenities of the city by undeveloped land, industrial uses, topography, and lack of appropriate street pattern.

2 It is further isolated and stigmatized by the contrast between the institutional buildings on site and the traditional neighborhood houses around it.

3 The street pattern fails to connect it adequately to major approach roads, making it difficult to create a good address.

4 By burying the streambed, the project created on-site problems, interrupted a natural feature, and lost an opportunity to link it to the rest of the city.

5 The configuration of open space separates rather than connects the neighborhoods.

Emerging urban design principles:

1 Build new neighborhood amenities as well as new houses that can serve to revitalize and connect with adjacent neighborhoods.

2 Restore the natural form of the land by re-opening the streambed and creating a linear park that can be the shared focus of many neighborhoods.

3 Create an interconnected network of streets and public open space, the focus of which is the new streambed park, which creates good addresses for residential development.

4 Provide a dignified setting for existing and proposed civic and religious buildings that ensures their central role in the life of the community.

5 Provide a mix of house types, and a mix of income of residents, with no distinction by tenure type or income.

6 Ensure high-quality architecture that responds to the best traditions of neighborhood design in the region.

7 Continue to involve residents, neighbors, civic leaders, and the financial and development community in the design process.

WAR STORY NO. 10

Cab drivers who say they can get you to the airport in five minutes really will! Wear your seatbelt.

ROBERT FREEDMAN

Each participant in a public process is given three green dots to locate best places and three red dots to identify worst places. The results are compiled to create a "good things" (in green)/"bad things" (in red) diagram.

Preparing For and Conducting a Four-Day, On-Site Charrette

The on-site charrette is meant to continue the process of consensus-building that began during Trip One. At this point in the process, we want to begin to move the client, their constituents, and the project team forward toward the development of specific community-supported urban design solutions. An intense, multi-day event, the on-site charrette is the focal point of this process. When well-conceived and well-executed, the charrette becomes a singularly powerful exercise by a community to design their community for the future.

One can't escape the obvious—it is easy to achieve consensus when all we are dealing with are generalizations and words. No one takes exception to a goal of making a good neighborhood, or a lively downtown, or of having the design solutions reflect the traditions of the place yet be forward-looking, too.

Turn those glittering generalities into concrete proposals, however, and oftentimes the fur begins to fly. When people start seeing specific visualizations of their stated goals, that's when the objections, resistance, personal preferences, and hidden agendas begin to show up in full force.

"We didn't think it should look like that!" "Why is everything so red?" (the color we use to depict the "not so good" things). "That doesn't look like it belongs here!" "I don't see how *that* is going to solve our problems." These are just a few of the comments we frequently hear in response to our first sketches.

That's why managing the logistics and staging the charrette for optimum effect is critical. Make no mistake—the on-site charrette is a piece of performance art. The space, the setup, the lighting must all lend a dramatic quality to the charrette. In a sense, this is community theater, and, to work its magic properly —that is, to draw the audience into the drama to produce the desired result (a common vision for the future of their community)—we must have all the logistical details nailed down tight.

The drawings must progress in a logical sequence of scale. Not only must they "read" from across the room, they must be arrayed in a manner that makes them approachable. As residents, municipal officials, business representatives and developers, the general public, and the media gather in the space, we want them to mix and mingle in small groups in front of each of the drawings. We want them to use the drawings as catalysts to discussion and to coalition. The charrette becomes the stage on which potential adversaries can align their respective interests and emerge with a cohesive plan.

Finally, food eases tension and can be an important component of a successful on-site charrette. Whether it's coffee and danish in the morning, sandwiches at lunch, or cookies and soft drinks throughout the day, food helps draw people into the process and soften their stridency. It's hard to be mean to your neighbor when your mouth is full.

The Flow of the Four-Day On-Site Charrette

Day One. Day One is a day for sharing the results of our data-gathering, analysis, and focus groups with the various constituencies affected by potential changes at the proposed site. Over the course of the day, we may present our findings several times to different groups of constituents. Each time, we want to know what the participants think about what we've uncovered and what ideas, suggestions, and concerns they each have. Our goal is to involve these individuals in the process, elicit their opinions, and record their input for use during the development of actual design alternatives during the remaining days of the charrette. Typically, we brief the media on Day One — and, because the event has been advertised as an open forum with the public welcome, we keep the doors open throughout the day so that people can wander in and out as they choose. As the day progresses, the team uses the input gathered during the day to begin drawing and coloring design alternatives directly onto copies of the base drawings, x-rays, and portraits we've brought with us.

Day Two. If it hasn't already been done on Day One, on Day Two, we set up the scale model for the site. Wood or plastic blocks that represent the various scales and styles of buildings that may be constructed on the site are unpacked, waiting for the process to begin to place them on the site in ways that respond to the input of the participants in this segment of the charrette.

WAR STORY NO. 11

If you use a copy service to reproduce your drawings, check to make sure they're not backwards before you take them to the charrette.

GREG WEIMERSKIRCH

Project team members are working in various parts of the room — the architects, illustrator, landscape architect, and others on the team are sketching away, much the way courtroom sketch artists draw during a trial.

At the same time, lively discussions are taking place throughout the room. Project team members encourage and subtly facilitate these conversations, exploring issues and options, problems and possibilities, with all assembled. As concerns surface, they are discussed and the drawings refined or redone as required.

Day Three. Early on Day Three, we need to touch base with the client. Then work on the drawings continues, and, when they are ready, the design team shares the preliminary designs and plans with the client and constituent representatives. The process of comment and refinement continues throughout the day. The open door policy encourages people to stop by, even if only for a few moments to check out what's going on. It's amazing what this creates in terms of energy, good will, and camaraderie.

Day Three concludes with a public meeting during which time the finished drawings, model, and plan are presented. Once the formal presentations have been made, we break into smaller groups to invite critique and additional discussion. A principal, project manager, or team member facilitates each of the small group discussions, and another member of the staff records audience comments on large easel pads. These pro and con comments are brought back to the office and used as input in preparing final project-specific urban design principles and design recommendations for the client.

Day Four. Day Four is spent in a debriefing meeting with the client group. At this critical meeting, a consensus is usually reached regarding the direction for the final plan.

During the charrette, a variety of ideas get presented (as illustrated by the Kimberly Park charrette excerpts presented here). The ideas for Kimberly Park were developed in response to what we heard throughout the process. Only by getting reactions to the color, shape, form, and image of a design direction are we able to effectively invent forms that respond to the many contexts and constituencies who will be served by the project.

WAR STORY NO. 12

Don't think that you know a city so well that you can drive home from the charrette at 1 a.m. without a map.

KIT McCULLOUGH

Kimberly Park Four-Day On-Site Charrette

On the first evening of the charrette, residents met us at a barbeque dinner outside the church. They talked to us about the history of the neighborhood, the strength of the churches surrounding the neighborhood, the sense of potential for the whole area. Our conversation with the residents revealed that many of the people who grew up in the neighborhood still get together every year to talk about old times. They call this gathering "The Pond." A pond was at the center of the universe for the neighborhood before the public housing was built and the stream was routed into an underground pipe. Our design evolved into the restoration of the stream as the centerpiece of a new neighborhood park system, restoring an element of "The Pond" and connecting the sense of the past with the future.

Before

After

The x-rays and the process identified three types of issues that needed to be resolved with the new design. These issues are illustrated on pages 118 and 119 as three pairs of x-rays, first the existing and then one with the design inserted.

Before

After

In the course of the charrette, many different design concepts emerged. By the third day, there was general consensus on an ideal overall form, one that re-established the stream-bed and created a linear park along it. The major open question was one of cost and feasibility. Is it really possible to make such a major change in the urban landscape within the constraints of this program? Therefore, the charrette concluded with two alternative designs:

Alternative One
Preferred Alternative

Peters Creek is restored as a natural streambed and is the central feature of a linear park, which is the principal public space in the neighborhood. A series of small-scale neighborhood streets provides direct access between new residential addresses and the new park. The street pattern connects to adjacent neighborhoods. The new development joins seamlessly with those neighborhoods and provides a focus of the entire area.

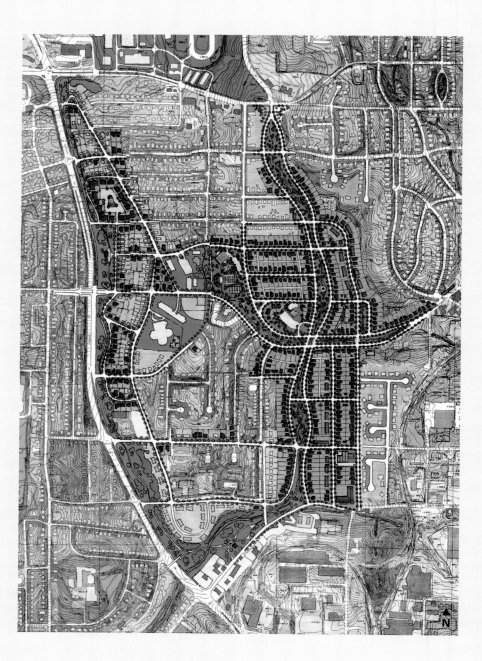

N

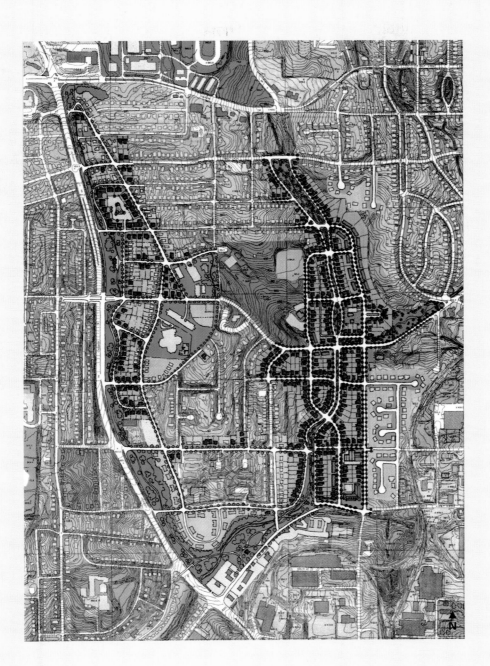

Alternative Two

The lower portion of Peters Creek is restored with a small park, but the northern portion remains in culvert. The street pattern is similar to the preferred alternative, and would serve to connect the new residential development to other neighborhoods and to the amenities in the area, and would provide good addresses for a wide range of houses.

Recommendations:

The Site

The barracks-like buildings of the public housing project separated the neighborhoods and isolated residents. In the proposed plan, parks and streets lined with houses connect neighborhood parks and schools to the adjacent neighborhoods.

Each new house, whether single-family, duplex, or triple, has a well-defined front yard, in some cases porches, and an architectural character based on local architectural styles.

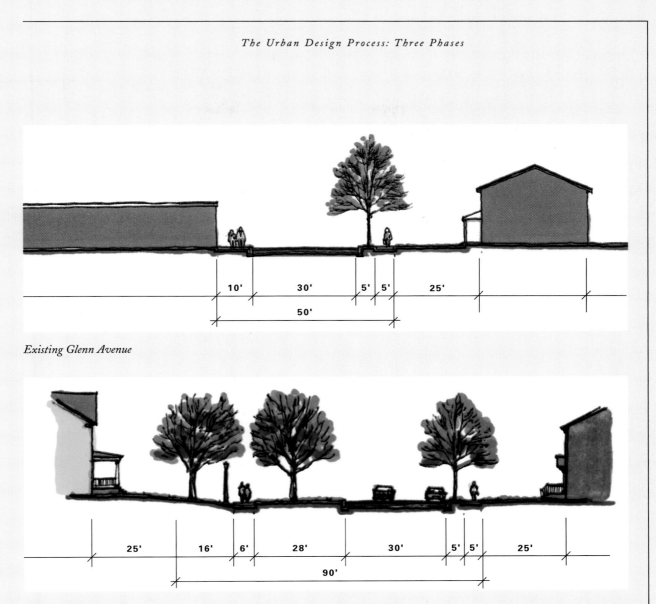

Existing Glenn Avenue

Proposed Glenn Avenue

Recommendations:

The correct design of streets includes all of the elements: the width of the cartway itself, the width of the sidewalk, the tree lawn, and the setback of the buildings. The existing street is an unfriendly street with the housing units facing a blank wall across the street.

The cartway is too wide and there is no tree lawn on one side. The proposed street is just wide enough for two-way traffic and parking on both sides, and the setbacks of houses follow patterns found on traditional neighborhood streets in the area.

Labeling and Filing X-Rays, Drawings, and Project Correspondence

Phase Two is a time of analysis and design exploration. It typically produces a rather extensive array of x-rays and conceptual drawings (e.g., plans, perspectives, sections, and diagrams). Some of these may need to be refined; all need to be properly labeled (including drawing title, readable street names, north arrows, etc.), catalogued, and assembled in working files — as hard copies and/or electronic files as appropriate.

UDA has developed file naming conventions and filing procedures to ensure that all work products are identified and archived properly so that they remain readily available for current project use as well as for future reference. As individual x-rays and drawings are developed, they should immediately be identified and catalogued. This applies to written project correspondence as well. It is far easier and less time consuming to follow these procedures as all materials are created rather than trying to accomplish this task as a big blitz at the end of a project. You'll find detailed filing procedures in Appendix A that will guide you through UDA's process.

Documenting the Charrette

Documenting the results of the on-site charrette is a critical component of Phase Two. By promptly recording, in writing, the input received during the charrette, you accomplish two important tasks. First, you capture all the information obtained in one document as part of the record of the process while it is still fresh in your mind. This becomes extremely useful in preparing an interim report to the client (if there is one — not all projects require an interim report), and when you get ready to prepare the final report at the end of Phase Three. Second, this documentation forms the foundation for launching into Phase Three: Deciding What to Do — Developing the Plan.

Developing an Interim Report

If the project scope includes an interim report, now is the appropriate time to prepare one. An interim report typically summarizes and discusses the significant information gathered during Phases One and Two, as well as the results of the on-site charrette. Depending on the level of clarity and definition achieved during the charrette, you may have one clearly emergent solution or several viable alternatives. The interim report sets these forth in a concise manner, discussing their relative merits vis-à-vis community expectations and aspirations. Typically, the report will be prepared in memo form and accompanied by the most pertinent drawings (e.g., plan, perspective, and aerial perspective drawings). UDA has established standard specifications for how drawings are to be mounted for presentation. The callouts on the drawing show UDA's standard specifications for labeling and mounting drawings to be used in presentations.

Circulating the Interim Report to the Client for Review

Once the interim report has been reviewed thoroughly in-house, it is sent to the client for review and comment.

Since our process is a highly participatory one — and depends on that for its ultimate success — we take client and community feedback very much to heart as we move forward with a project. While the comments listed are specific to Kimberly Park (a project for which we did not prepare an interim report), the comments give you a sense of the type of client feedback we often receive and need to be prepared to respond to effectively. These particular comments and ideas emerged at the very end of the Kimberly Park charrette and during a number of discussions among various client, consultant, and community groups.

The comments were then passed along to us by phone or in meetings. Note also: While these comments are being presented here as "typical feedback" for this stage of a project, such comments may occur throughout the process. It's important to continue to capture and carefully consider their significance as you refine the designs and develop the plan during Phase Three.

Key comments included:

→ We think opening up the covered creek (daylighting the creek) is a good idea.

→ The community strongly prefers the alternative that opens up the entire creek and will create the most change to the urban structure of the area, but we're concerned about its feasibility and cost.

→ We're concerned about the number of low-income families who could remain.

→ Some of us are really uncomfortable about demolishing so many buildings.

→ Changes to the existing parks might result in less parkland. Our goal was to do a 1-for-1 trade in the reconfiguration.

→ We really like the image of the new neighborhood.

We're now ready to embark on Phase Three.

PHASE THREE: DECIDING WHAT TO DO
Developing the Plan

Phase Three is the part of the process where we use everything we have learned from our client, community representatives, and the consulting team to zero in on a preferred alternative. Phase Three consists of the following steps that culminate in the production and delivery of a final report to the client:

→ Assigning and coordinating testing by the consulting team

→ Conducting an in-house charrette

→ Conducting the second on-site charrette (or mini-charrette) to gather comments and achieve consensus

→ Selecting the preferred alternative

→ Developing additional images

→ Preparing presentation materials and final design documents

→ Producing the final report

→ Defining next steps

Assigning and Coordinating the Testing by the Consulting Team

As we begin Phase Three, we often ask consultants to review and comment on the interim report—or, in the absence of an interim report, on the viability of those concepts that have been identified as most promising by our clients and their constituents. Frequently at this stage, some final testing of the ideas is desirable and, if so, the appropriate subconsultant(s) are given those assignments. Here's what was done to test the concepts for Kimberly Park and the influence that testing had on design changes for the project:

→ A major effort was undertaken to test the realities of daylighting the creek and to ensure that it would work technically. Engineers tested whether water would flow on the slopes. Some actually ran uphill!

→ The landscape architects and engineers checked the grading to make sure the house lot and block layouts and streets worked with the topography. Streets are always tricky because conventional city standards call for streets designed for higher speeds than are desirable in residential neighborhoods. This causes the roads to be too wide, with too much change to existing contours, thereby destroying the character of the site, and resulting in a neighborhood with fast drivers and impersonal streets. This battle was fought and a good compromise reached.

→ To create the new park configuration, it was necessary to research property ownership and make sure that private property could be acquired and traded for public land.

→ A general market study was done prior to the charrette. Results of that study were used to establish the market basis for a program and set the preliminary direction for developing the urban design. In the charrette, the only rental housing depicted was in the renovated public housing buildings; everything else shown was home-ownership units. During testing, it became clear that there were more single-family houses for sale than the market could absorb. A developer was then hired who had a different development program — i.e., more rental properties. Market studies indicated that these rental units would have to be all new construction to be marketable. This would require total demolition of the existing buildings. The residents were nervous until they saw the designs and realized that the program actually increased the number of public housing units in the mix, thus enabling more people to stay in the project. New construction also made it possible to have more market-rate rental units for a better mix. The net result was more rental buildings overall — quite a change to the preliminary site plan!

Conducting a Second In-House Charrette

Frequently, an in-house charrette will produce better understanding of the issues and refine ideas further before you hold the second on-site charrette in the community. Our consultants generally participate in some or all of the in-house charrette and, frequently, a client representative will be present. When a client representative is not present at this event, close communication is maintained via phone and e-mail to ensure that emerging ideas remain on course.

This is the best time to identify and explore with the client any major issues that remain either unaddressed or insufficiently addressed by the options proposed. It is not unusual as you move through this process to discover that some changes to the design concepts are required to meet client and community objectives. If such additional work is required, the principal and project manager will assess what is necessary and assign the tasks to the appropriate project team members.

For Kimberly Park, these changes and further developments consisted of:

→ Reorienting the street grid to accommodate the new rental program. As it happens, this resulted in a much better plan because every street now ends in a park.

→ Remixing the site to have 70% rental and 30% home-ownership units

→ Adding amenities and including tot lots, walking trails, and pedestrian bridges

These ideas are then taken to the second on-site charrette and further refined within the context of that community forum.

Conducting the Second On-Site Charrette to Gather Comments and Achieve Consensus

The second on-site charrette is organized in much the same manner as the first was, making whatever modifications to the setup or agenda that might seem worthwhile based on what worked successfully (or didn't) during the first charrette. Sometimes the second on-site charrette is a mini-charrette, when circumstances permit us to achieve what is necessary in less than the three to four days normally consumed by a full charrette. The principal and the project manager, in conjunction with the client, set the agenda and logistics for the second charrette and then brief the participants on how to proceed.

Since we often present more than one option to clients, an important part of our role during the second charrette is to facilitate communication so that all stakeholders can move toward consensus. Our role is to gather and compile comments, eliciting as much response as possible from participants to the ideas being proposed.

Our objectives are to:

→   Present the ideas and options to the community

→   Clarify any aspects of the concepts that are still unclear to stakeholders

→   Probe for any remaining significant concerns that could delay or jeopardize the success of the project

→   Get a clear understanding of which concepts the community prefers

→   Reach consensus on these ideas through this public process

Selecting the Preferred Alternative

Consensus-building facilitates the selection of the preferred alternative. It is not the urban designers who determine the preferred alternative, but rather our clients in conjunction with all the stakeholders who must live with (and should benefit from) the alternative selected.

Typically, the preferred alternative arises from a combination of the proposed ideas. This was the case for Kimberly Park. The preferred alternative ultimately developed into the final plan with six major recommendations:

1   Construct a new street grid within the project that would create a traditional residential neighborhood through block formation as well as calm traffic through the site.

2   Provide a mix of housing types that would encourage the development of Kimberly Park as a mixed-income neighborhood while creating a strong base of newly constructed, attractive, subsidized and low-income rental units that would enable current residents to remain in the neighborhood.

3   Through building types and style, create an image of the neighborhood that would be in harmony, in scale and character, with adjacent neighborhoods.

4   Create more public green space through a proposed new park.

5   Reconnect the neighborhood to parks, amenities, and jobs.

6   Build an addition onto the existing Martin Luther King Center to augment community-oriented facilities and services.

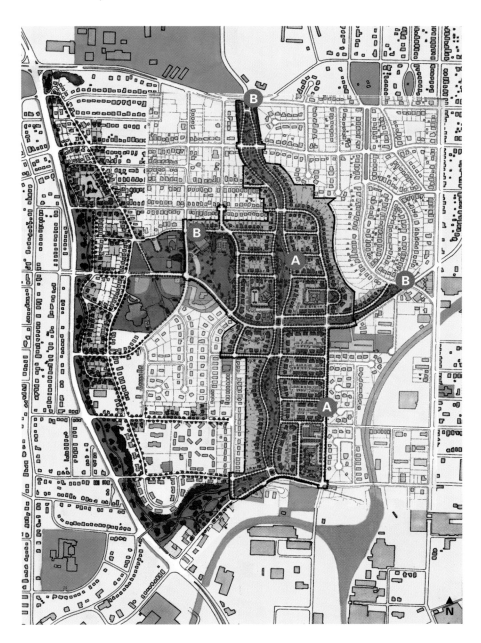

Final Plan

Peters Creek is restored as a natural streambed and is the central feature of a linear park, which is the principal public space in the neighborhood. A series of small-scale neighborhood streets provide direct access between new residential addresses and the new park. The street pattern connects to adjacent neighborhoods. The new development joins seamlessly with those neighborhoods and provides a focus for the entire area.

For the final plan, additional modifications were made to the preferred alternative:

→ Street grid was modified to connect streets to park **A**

→ Modifications to parks on north, east, and west **B**

→ Changes in building types due to developer's program (the developer was not part of the original planning)

Developing Additional Images

During Phase Three, new images are often created. These must also be entered into the system and filed according to the filing conventions detailed in Appendix A. Although not everything amassed will necessarily be used in the final report, this is the ideal time to select and file any new or revised drawings that were not automatically entered into the archiving system as they were developed.

Subconsultants (e.g., traffic planners, civil engineers, and landscape architects) often provide us with images for the report. These should be filed at this time as well. The principal-in-charge and the project manager will help select the most desirable images.

Preparing Presentation Materials and Final Design Documents

UDA's presentation materials typically consist of a slide show and mounted drawings, which are used at our final presentation to the client at a public forum and wrap-up session before the final report is prepared.

Presentation materials will vary from project to project. This list for Kimberly Park is typical:

→ Winston-Salem City Map

→ Site Map

→ Existing Zoning Map

→ Phasing/Demolition/Relocation Plan

→ Series of Before-and-After Eye-Level Perspectives

→ Context (plan view) — Existing Conditions

→ Context (plan view) — Proposals

→ Before-and-After X-Rays

→ Streets

→ Parks/Open Space

→ Building Coverage

→ Site Plan — Existing Conditions

→ Site Plan Proposals

→ Before-and-After Aerials

→ Proposed Building Uses Plan

→ Public Improvements Plan

→ Streetscapes/Parks and Open Space Plan

→ Street Designs and Cross Sections

→ Building Plans and Elevations

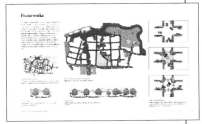

The drawings on the next several pages, while considerably reduced in size, give a bird's-eye view of the intent, content, and style we employ for these presentation materials.

Producing the Final Report

UDA urban design projects conclude with the publication of a final report. UDA considers the images that illustrate both the process and the ideas created in that process to be the most valuable of our products.

However, for many projects, an elaborate report is not necessary. In those cases, we prepare a series of either 8½" x 11" or 11" x 17" pages with images and captions. This is accompanied with a typed memorandum summarizing the process and a bound collection of the working documents produced during the course of the project. The 11" x 17" pages are designed to be printed as 24" x 36" exhibit boards.

Typical 11" x 17" Report
The above pages illustrate a format for an 11" x 17" report.

For more extensive reports, the development of a final report typically proceeds in the following sequence:

The Outline. The principal and/or project manager prepares an outline of the final report. This should be sent to the client for review and approval. A copy should also be sent to the firm's publications team, with a note alerting them that a report is being prepared and the likely timetable so that they can factor the assignment into their work schedule.

SELECTED IMAGES FROM THE FINAL REPORT

Recommendations:

Parks and Open Space

The proposal re-opens the buried streambed to create a linear park that connects the site to other neighborhoods. The new park, proposed to be named Peters Creek Park, also links existing parks and institutions in a continuous network of public open space that provides amenities throughout the community.

Existing Parks and Open Space

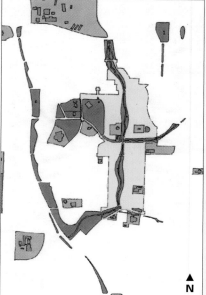

Proposed Parks and Open Space

Recommendations:

Streets Network

The new linear park is bounded by neighborhood-scale, narrow-cartway park drives—one side for each direction of travel—with parallel parking along it. This parkway extends to the north to connect to the college campus and major arterials. It is the central spine for a new network of small-scale residential streets that connect to adjacent communities on both sides of the site. It creates a series of attractive, new residential addresses.

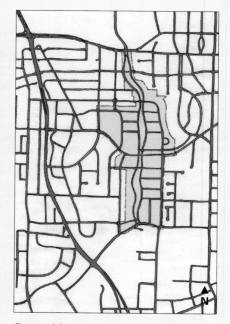

Existing Streets Network

Proposed Streets Network

SELECTED IMAGES FROM THE FINAL REPORT

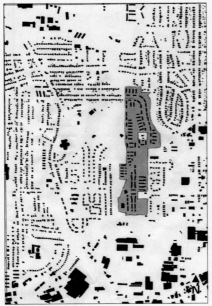

Existing Building Coverage

Proposed Building Coverage

Recommendations:

Buildings
The new interconnected network of parks and open space provides a series of addresses along which traditionally scaled houses will be built. They include single-family houses, double houses, triple houses, and small apartment houses.

Existing Perspective of Peters Creek Park

Recommendations:

Peters Creek Park Today
A three-acre parking lot in the middle of Kimberly Park was built over the creek and divides the community, and is a waste-land and a public safety problem for residents.

Peters Creek Park Tomorrow
The creek is re-opened and is the focus of a gracious neighborhood park lined with new houses.

Proposed Perspective of Peters Creek Park

119

SELECTED IMAGES FROM THE FINAL REPORT

Recommendations:
The before eye-level view (bottom) graphically demonstrates both the barren, inhuman character of the public housing project and negative impact of retaining walls and other poorly conceived site amenities. This is then transformed (above) by the reconstruction into a traditional neighborhood street.

SELECTED IMAGES FROM THE FINAL REPORT

Recommendations:
The existing project was developed with a series of artificial terraces in order to accommodate the standard, barracks-like buildings. The new development (above) will use smaller-scale structures that can comfortably fit on a natural slope and create a good neighborhood street.

The outline should include a list of all the images that will be contained in the report. (The materials identified above for Kimberly Park are typical of the UDA X-Rays and images contained in our final report. Any additional images that may be required will be identified by either the principal- or project-manager-in-charge.)

Each drawing serves a specific purpose — to illustrate and explain a key aspect of the design. Succinct captions (developed during the text development process for the final report) focus the reader on the essential point being made by each image.

The Dummy. When the outline has been revised and approved by the client, the principal and/or project manager prepares a dummy of the report, page by page, with actual images identified on each page, as well as spaces for the proposed text. This becomes the general road map that guides the publications team in developing the final layout.

The dummy should identify whether images (especially the master plan drawing) are horizontal, vertical, or square in format. Where cropping an image is desired or required, crop marks should be indicated on a hard copy of the drawing that is given to the publications team for reference.

UDA's approach is to be heavy on images and light on copy. A typical report runs between 30 and 50 pages.

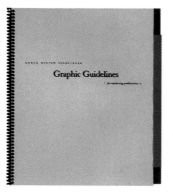

More Images. Often, in the process of preparing the dummy, we identify images that are missing or images that should be revised. The principal and/or project manager will meet with the project team members to go over the dummy and to assign drawing and/or photographing tasks. This work is best done as a charrette over several days with the team concentrating solely on this project so that consistency, coordination, and cohesiveness of detail across the array of drawings can be achieved.

All scanned images, both the previously scanned images and the new ones to be used in the report, should now be placed on a Zip™ disk or CD with the file names cross-referenced to the dummy.

The Text. The principal and/or project manager, working with the dummy as a guide, will prepare the draft text at the same time that the image charrette is occurring. This enables us to adjust images and text concurrently to ensure that they are consistent with one another.

Some of the text will be prepared by subconsultants, such as traffic, market, or landscape consultants. Subconsultants need to be alerted to the production schedule for the report, as they will be required to meet the same production schedule.

The text need not be formatted in any special way, nor does it need to fit exactly the space designated in the dummy. These issues will be addressed during layout and editing. What's most important now is just to get the words down in a continuous text with appropriate headings. Try to the maximum extent possible to let the images carry the day, not the words.

An Executive Summary is written once the full text of the report has been drafted and edited.

Printing. Now is the time to meet with the supplier selected for the project. The printer will need a copy of the dummy, hard copy of the text for reference, and a Zip disk containing all the scanned images and the digital files of the text. Some gaps may still remain in the text, but these should be kept to a minimum (ideally no more than 10% of the total text). Gaps in the text should be clearly identified on the hard copy to alert the supplier to the locations where additional text will be forthcoming. The images on the Zip disk will need to be labeled and cross-referenced to the images on the dummy pages.

The meeting with the supplier should not take place until the dummy, the draft text, and the Zip disk with text and cross-referenced digital images are all ready to release. The entire team—the principal, the project manager, and the interns—should attend the meeting with the printer.

The Rough Draft. Within a few weeks, the printer will return a black and white (laser) copy of the draft report for review and updating. This should be redlined immediately and sent back to the printer with whatever new text and images are needed.

The First Client Draft. The printer makes the changes in the rough draft and provides proofs—usually one color proof and one black and white master—to be checked and proofread. Return changes to the printer for incorporation into the master file. UDA requires two bound color copies and one unbound black and white master. The project manager sends one color copy and the black and white copy to the client for distribution and review.

The Final Client Draft. After the client's review comments are received, additional editing may or may not be required. Once that has been determined and any editing done, a meeting with the printer should take place to discuss the changes to the text, images, and labeling, and to provide direction for the final version, which reflects the comments of the client and UDA. One final black and white proof is sent to the client for review and comment.

The Final Report. The principal and/or project manager reviews the client comments and checks the final report one last time; an in-house editor may provide a final review. The project manager consolidates all changes onto a master copy of the report, and this is given to the printer for production of the final document. The final report may be given to the client in digital form, multiple printed copies, or a combination, depending on the arrangement with the client and the budget. Each project is different in this respect.

Some Helpful Tips for Producing Reports

→   From the beginning of the project, keep in mind that the report is the final product. Drawings, photographs, and slides are the raw material for the report, so draw them, develop them, label them, store them, and protect them with that end product in view.

→   Text is most potent when tied to images. Too much text becomes unreadable.

→   Well-written captions on drawings and photos can often take the place of a whole sentence or paragraph in the text.

→   Labeling on drawings that may work in a slide presentation may be difficult to see in a reduced form in a report. We often leave out street names and north arrows on presentation drawings. However, they must appear on the scanned images used in the report!

→   Make a plan, at the beginning of Phase Three, to prepare the dummy, write the text, and prepare any new drawings in a dedicated, concentrated effort (a charrette) over several days. It's the most efficient and effective way to develop the materials for the final report. You can't imagine how much frustration and hair pulling you'll avoid by diligently following this piece of advice!

Making the Final Presentation

Clients often ask for a final presentation on a project. This may occur before or after delivery of the final report. The presentation generally consists of a public slide presentation, followed by a question-and-answer session and discussion. Sometimes break-out sessions are included, using the same format as that used during the charrettes. Usually, there is also a final meeting with the steering committee following the public presentation.

The final plan embodies the ideas that have emerged, and that have been distilled, throughout the process.

FINAL PRESENTATION DRAWINGS

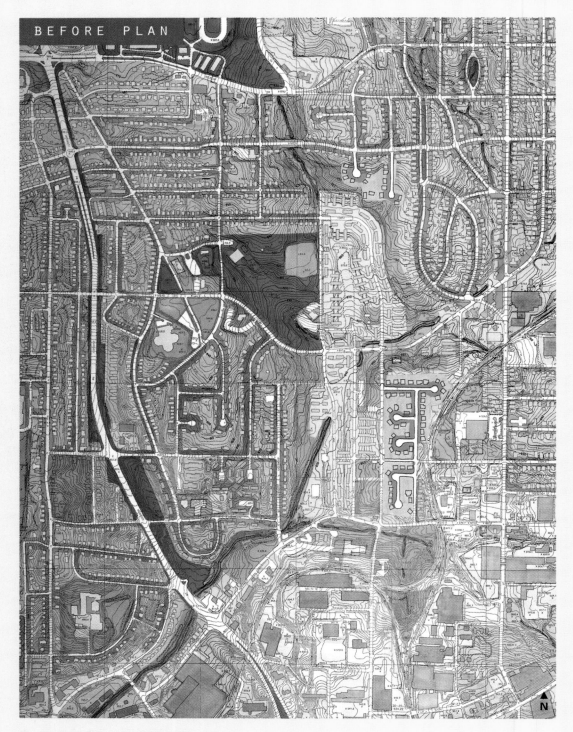

BEFORE PLAN

Portrait of Existing Conditions

FINAL PRESENTATION DRAWINGS

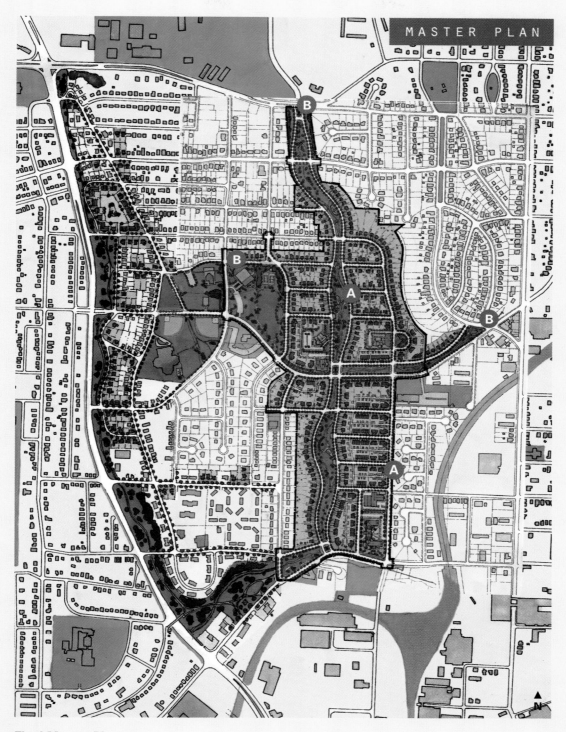

MASTER PLAN

Final Master Plan

Kimberly Park

Project Sheets

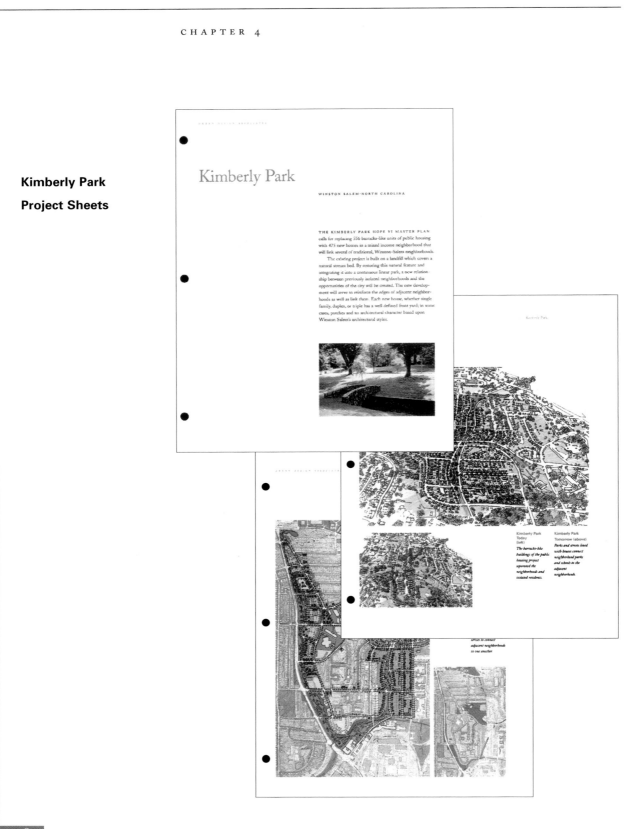

URBAN DESIGN ASSOCIATES

Kimberly Park

WINSTON SALEM·NORTH CAROLINA

THE KIMBERLY PARK HOPE VI MASTER PLAN
calls for replacing 556 barracks-like units of public housing
with 475 new homes in a mixed income neighborhood that
will link several of traditional, Winston-Salem neighborhoods.

The existing project is built on a landfill which covers a
natural stream bed. By restoring this natural feature and
integrating it into a continuous linear park, a new relationship between previously isolated neighborhoods and the
opportunities of the city will be created. The new development will serve to reinforce the edges of adjacent neighborhoods as well as link them. Each new house, whether single
family, duplex, or triple has a well defined front yard; in some
cases, porches and an architectural character based upon
Winston Salem's architectural styles.

Kimberly Park
Today
(left)
*The barracks-like
buildings of the public
housing project
separated the
neighborhoods and
isolated residents.*

Kimberly Park
Tomorrow (above)
*Parks and streets lined
with houses connect
neighborhood parks
and schools to the
adjacent
neighborhoods.*

serves to connect
adjacent neighborhoods
to one another

Project Sheets

Every UDA project is also summarized on a UDA Project Sheet, which we use for marketing purposes. This is done while the project is fresh in everyone's minds. The project manager is responsible for gathering the information and writing the text. Since all the images are already in the computer, the project manager needs only to select four or five key images, create captions, and write a brief paragraph (three or four sentences) describing the essence and the highlights of the project.

UDA's marketing coordinator, using a standard design template created for that purpose, creates the project sheet, and consults the project manager and principal-in-charge for final review. The principal-in-charge reviews the project sheet before it becomes a part of the marketing file.

Next Steps

While the final report is the culmination of our services on an urban design project, it often does not conclude our involvement with the project. Frequently we are retained to help our client obtain the formal approvals necessary to proceed with project development, and we are often involved with aspects of the implementation. We may be retained as an ongoing consultant to advise our client during the implementation process. We may be engaged to develop more detailed urban design drawings or to focus on specific sites within the plan. We are often hired to create pattern books (the subject of Chapter 5) as a tool for both project marketing and building design/development purposes. In addition, UDA's architectural services are often sought for the design of both key and prototype buildings. Chapter 6 presents UDA's architectural design process.

MR. POTATO HEAD™

A classic children's toy, Mr. Potato Head provides several choices for eyes, noses, mouths, and ears, enabling children to create a great variety of different "people" by the choices they make among the available facial features. The basic shape is pretty clear—a potato. And the general positioning of each feature is known—two eyes go on the upper part of the front, two ears symmetrically placed on the sides, the nose in the mid portion of the front, the mouth somewhere below it.

Pattern books work in much the same way. The massing patterns provide a set of basic shapes (the potato). Windows and doors, like eyes and ears, have their correct place on the facades. Porches and other special features (the noses) have a prominent place in the front, and the main door (the mouth) finds its place underneath them.

CHAPTER

The UDA Pattern Book Process: Four Phases

THE PROCESS FOR CREATING A UDA PATTERN BOOK

UDA is often a member of a much larger development team trying to ensure the quality of the built work. We may have been the master planners. When we are not, we are often teamed with the master planners to bridge the gap between two-dimensional planning and three-dimensional implementation.

Our role is that of interpreter, inventor, and liaison between urban design, developer, and builder. In that capacity, we translate the architectural style into current building practices and the hidden patterns of traditional neighborhoods and towns into current lotting and zoning requirements. Our approach is to revive the tradition of creating pattern books for builders.

Reviving the Pattern Book Tradition

As the United States developed through westward expansion, settlers built houses and towns on the frontier of the wilderness, often far away from civilization. The rapid growth of the nation resulted in a series of building booms, in which thousands of houses were built each decade in each community. And yet, the results of this rapid construction are carefully crafted houses along beautifully landscaped streets or around lovingly maintained public parks and squares. Houses in a variety of architectural styles have beautifully proportioned and ornamented

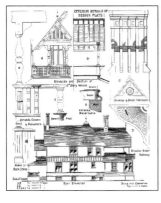

Examples of pattern book pages originally published by William T. Comstock in 1881 are typical of the books used by American builders through the early part of the 20th century.

facades. Windows, doors, roof forms, porches all follow complex and sophisticated principles of design. Equally impressive is the balance that was achieved between the individual expression of each house and the harmony with which they work together to create community form.

How was such a sophisticated level of design maintained across so wide an area in so short a period of time? An important part of the answer is pattern books — builders' handbooks that contained principles for design and design details that presented clearly and concisely the architectural and other elements of traditional styles. These books are the direct descendants of the handbooks that have been, since ancient Roman times, the means by which architects have passed along their knowledge of design to builders in remote places. Pattern books set the rules, but each builder found ways of interpreting them, elaborating them, or even bending them. The result has been the exquisite balance of individual expression and unity that is present in America's finest traditional neighborhoods — where individual homes have their unique characteristics, yet relate to their neighbors in ways that create a sense of community.

In the second half of the 19th century, pattern books became more than just a builder's tool; they became part of a marketing program, enabling prospective homebuyers to see a variety of house styles through realistic sketches of the finished results, along with the floor plans and key details for each style. Some pattern books were catalogues of parts (doors, windows, etc.), and in others entire houses could be ordered. The pattern book tradition continued until World War II. After the war, architects became interested in the Modernist style and lost interest in traditional architectural patterns. In the great post-war building boom, pattern books fell into disuse.

Consequently, today's builders often operate without access to the conventions that historically enabled individual buildings to create urban space. New technologies have liberated building processes and form, but have failed to provide a set of principles for creating buildings of scale. Architecture, sadly, has abandoned home-building and much of the traditional vocabularies.

Our goal in developing 21st-century pattern books is to help restore among builders, designers, and homebuyers the consensus that once existed and that enabled them to create the beautiful historic neighborhoods we so admire. By reviving this tradition and adapting it to 21st-century technology, the building industry will once again be able to create neighborhoods that celebrate the values we share as a society.

On any given project, our goal is to ensure that the architects and builders engaged to create homes for that site have the tool they need to design houses that will create the quality and the character of neighborhood and public spaces envisioned in the urban design. Like its 19th-century ancestors, UDA's pattern book is designed to be an effective marketing tool. Because pattern books relate the architectural patterns to the marketing themes for a given development, the book enables prospective homebuyers to "see" the overall vision for the neighborhood and appreciate how their new home will fit within that context. Rather than being a "code" that tells people what they can't do, pattern books help homebuyers envision what they can do — what their new dream house can look like. As such, pattern books are proactive, providing a collection of details and methods for building houses that spark the imagination and support the design concept for the neighborhood or town.

UDA intends pattern books to be viewed as a "kit of parts" that gives designers and builders the flexibility to create a wide range of houses while still maintaining the distinct characteristics of traditional neighborhood design inherent in that region. How we understand space, as well as the specific manifestation of an architectural style, often varies in local interpretation from one region to another. Sensitivity to such considerations is an integral part of our approach to pattern book development.

UDA Pattern Book examples >

THE STRUCTURE OF THE TYPICAL UDA PATTERN BOOK

UDA pattern books typically consist of the following sections:

→ **Overview**

→ **Community Patterns**

→ **Architectural Patterns**

→ **Landscape Patterns**

→ **Appendix**

Overview

The first section in each pattern book identifies the essential qualities and key patterns in the community within which the pattern book will be used. Research is conducted using historic documents, photography, and field measurements. The collected material is analyzed to identify repeating patterns, including the dimensions of streets and sidewalks, setbacks for buildings, architectural styles, dominant materials and colors, and landscape palettes used in both public spaces and on private property.

The process then identifies the patterns most appropriate for the development, whether new or infill development. This is often done in a public process or one that includes many members of the development team and community as described in Chapter 4.

For residential development, we often describe the essential attributes of the house type that responds to both local traditions and to the housing market.

While there are general qualities and patterns common to all of these examples, it is the way in which they are adapted and applied in local applications that creates the unique richness of American urbanism.

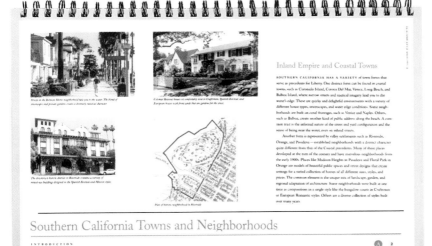

Sample Overview page from the Liberty Pattern Book

OVERVIEW

Community Patterns

Using research on local building traditions, this section describes the essential qualities of community space, the different building types, and how they are placed on their lots. The desired forms of streets and public spaces are described in plan view, as well as in sections indicating setbacks, facade properties, building height, and the character of the landscape treatment in both the public and private areas. Patterns for individual lots define the location of buildings, their volume, and areas for special design attention.

This section also describes and illustrates different addresses within the community. For example, each distinct address may be described on a page with a plan of lots having specific house placement criteria for that particular neighborhood. An eye-level perspective and a street section generally accompany the plan drawing to help create a full picture of the intent.

Sample Community
Patterns page from the
Baxter Pattern Book

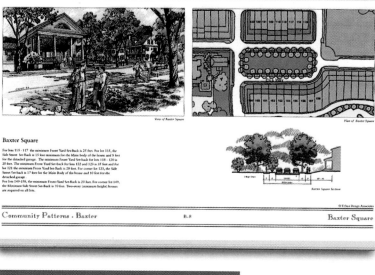

COMMUNITY PATTERNS

Architectural Patterns

The Architectural Patterns section defines the architectural style(s) selected for the project. For each architectural style, this section consists of six pages. The first page describes the essential qualities of the style. On the succeeding pages, patterns for the elements of that particular style are identified and described. Here again, we have crafted a kind of assembly kit, consisting of the basic massing of the house, on which windows and doors are placed, and to which special elements such as porches can be added, with a palette of materials and colors that are appropriate for that style.

On the following pages, an example of one style section from the pattern book prepared for a new town in Southern California is used to illustrate this system.

Sample Architectural Patterns page from the Liberty Pattern Book

History and Character

The history and key characteristics of the style are described in order to identify the essential elements that should be respected and built correctly. In any building process, there is a limit to the number of different aspects that can be controlled, so it is critical to ask for the ones that are most important. Four to six of these attributes are listed, illustrated, and described. The details on succeeding pages show how to design buildings that have these attributes.

In Southern California, the use of styles is more complex than in other regions of the country. A prevalent style in the region in which Liberty is located is a form of the Classical style, but with such a wide range of interpretations of Classical vocabularies that it includes houses that have much in common with Colonial Revival houses. In the pattern book, we have called this the Liberty Classic style. Its attributes include simple volumes, symmetrical composition of windows within each volume, simplified Classical details, and multi-paned windows with wide proportions.

Pages 138 through 143:
Sample Architectural Patterns pages from the Liberty Pattern Book

A simple symmetrical house in Orange with a full front porch

The symmetrical arrangement of windows and dormers creates a classical composition for this Classical house in Pasadena.

This house in Pasadena is a good example of horizontal proportions and the use of special windows.

Early twentieth century Colonial Revival house rendering

History and Character

THE LIBERTY CLASSIC is based on Colonial Revival styles that were prevalent throughout the country in the early 1900s. The Colonial Revival style is evident in many California towns and cities. Interesting renditions can be found in the Los Angeles area, including Madison Heights in Pasadena. Valley communities, such as Riverside and Orange, also have a diverse collection of period houses designed in the Colonial Revival style.

The Colonial Revival style is based on Classical design principles followed in the Colonial period in this country. The interpretations, however, are often regional in character. The Southern California examples include many houses with full front porches, Dutch Colonial renditions and unusual color use on the facade and architectural elements. Cornices are often deep, with extended overhangs and brackets along the soffit on the main body and the porches.

The houses are composed of simple forms with well-proportioned windows and door surrounds. These are often more horizontal in appearance with special windows appearing in the center of the house over the front door.

Essential Elements of the Liberty Classic

1 Simple, straightforward volumes with one-story side wings and porches added to make more complex shapes.

2 A symmetrical composition of doors and windows.

3 Simplified versions of Classical details and columns, often with robust and exotic Classical orders such as Ionic and Corinthian used in the porch element.

4 Multi-pane windows that are wide in proportion usually with 6 over 6 or 6 over 1 pane patterns.

Colonial Revival, Madison Heights neighborhood, Pasadena, California

Liberty Classic

ARCHITECTURAL PATTERNS

C   I

Massing and Composition

The massing of the house includes a main body in which the front door is located, and, in many instances, side wings for more complex houses. Patterns for massing establish the roof pitch, height, and overall form of the buildings. For example, the Liberty Classic style has a variety of roof forms that consist of combinations of a few basic forms such as a hip, gable, and gambrel. Facade composition, especially the placement of windows, is closely related to building massing. The relationship of windows within the main body of the house should relate to its basic volume, whether a simple rectangular form or a more complex one.

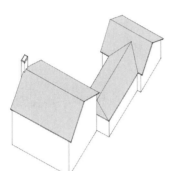

Massing Diagrams

A *Two-story basic*   B *Two-story front hip gable*   C *Two-story gable L*   D *Two-story box L*   E *One-and-one-half-story gambrel*   F *Two-story basic with add-on*

Massing and Composition

Massing

A   Two-story basic
Hipped or side-gabled rectangular volume. Hip roof pitch is typically 5 in 12 and gable roof pitch is 7 in 12. One-story temple front or hip front porches, placed symmetrically on the front facade. Two-story center porches are also permitted. Although porches are most often one-fifth the length of the main body, they may also be three-fifths or the entire length of the front facade.

B   Two-story front hip gable
Hipped or front-gabled rectangular volume. Hip roof pitch is typically 7 in 12 and gable roof pitch is 8 in 12. As with the basic massing, symmetrically placed gabled and/or hipped front porches are common. Porches may be either one- or two-story. Two-story porches are integral and are reserved for front-gabled houses between 24 and 30 feet wide.

C   Two-story gable L
Cross-gabled volume with an 8 in 12 gable facing the street. Cross gable has a lower slope. The width of the gable facing the street is typically half that of the main body for houses up to 36 feet wide and two-fifths that of the main body for houses 36 feet and over. This massing typically accommodates a continuous porch with shed roof located between the legs of the L.

D   Two-story box L
Hipped roof box with a two-story bay added to both the front and side. The bays shall have either a gabled roof with a 7 in 12 pitch or more commonly a hipped roof with a 5 in 12 pitch. Ideal for corner houses, this massing invites an L-shaped corner porch between the two bays.

E   One-and-one-half-story gambrel
Rectangular volume with a gambrel roof parallel to the street. Roof pitch is nearly vertical on the lower slope and 4 to 6 in 12 at the top. One-story temple front porches centered on the front facade are typical. Porches extending three-fifths or the entire length of the front facade are also permitted.

F   Two-story basic with add-on
Two-story main body with a gable or hip roof parallel to the street. An 'add-on' is usually a full- or partial-width one-story forward-projecting wing with similar roof form.

Facade Composition

Classic facade composition is characterized by a symmetrical and balanced placement of doors and windows. Standard windows most often occur as singles, or in pairs. Entrance doors are generally located in the corner of narrow houses and center of wide houses.

Liberty Classic

C   2

Massing and Eave Details

The massing of the house is articulated with eave and soffit details that are particular to each style. In the Liberty Classic example, the roof pitch is relatively shallow at 5 in 12. The roof overhang varies but can be as much as 2 feet, with wide but shallow brackets. Complex forms are created by adding side wings to the basic volume of the main body. This page also includes a wall section indicating both ceiling and window head heights.

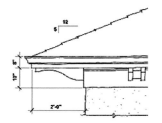

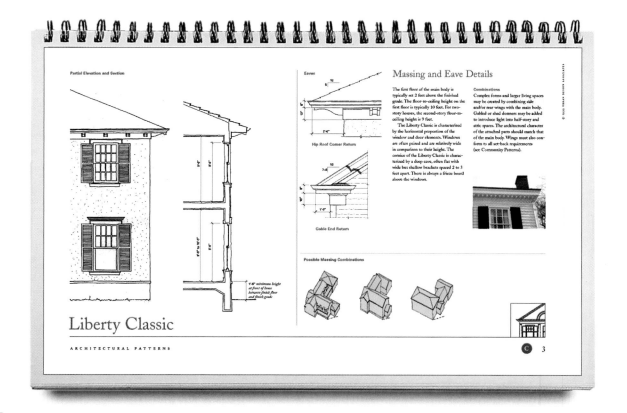

Windows and Doors

The proportion and profile of windows are essential attributes of each style presented. They are the most visible, figural elements of a house, and our eyes are drawn to them. The pattern book establishes both the proportions and the principles for placing them on the mass of the house.

For example, the Liberty Classic style uses two basic window types — a 6 over 6 and a 6 over 1. Ground-floor windows are taller than second-floor ones. Special windows include angled bays, arched windows, and a picture window. Correct door designs are illustrated, including the standard door and more complex ones with sidelights and ornamental door surrounds.

Porches

Each style is associated with a series of special elements. The porch is the special element most associated with the Liberty Classic style. Porches can be either one or two stories tall and can have a variety of roof and column configurations. This page indicates the way in which porches are placed on the various massing types of the style, and also includes a typical porch design to indicate the correct detailing for this style.

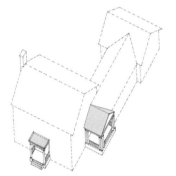

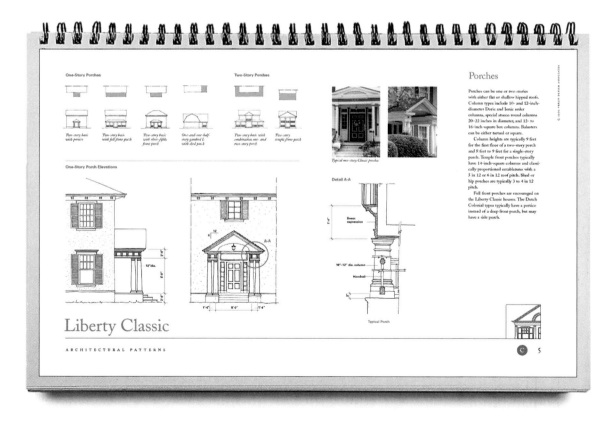

Liberty Classic

Materials, Colors, and Possibilities

A materials list is provided and illustrated in a large-scale partial elevation that includes some key details. Appropriate color palettes are specified, as well as appropriate application of these colors to the various parts of the house.

A number of possible house elevations are illustrated on this page. They all use the patterns that have been described on the previous five pages. They demonstrate the extraordinarily wide range of possible house designs that can be created by using combinations of the massing patterns, facade compositions, windows, doors, special elements, materials, and colors of the Liberty Classic style. These are all single-family houses. When the same elements of style are applied to other building types such as townhouses, small apartments, and duplexes, the possibilities multiply further. Typically, in each development, there are at least three different architectural styles. As a result, the new neighborhoods that are built with this approach have the diversity and richness of traditional, well-established ones.

Possibilities

Materials, Colors, and Possibilities

Materials

Siding: Stucco, wood, fiber cement board, or shingles.

Roofing: Cedar shakes; asphalt or fiberglass shingles with a heavy profile to mimic natural materials. Concrete tile not permitted.

Windows: Energy-efficient wood, PVC-clad, aluminum-clad, or aluminum, with external divided lights (⅞-inch muntins).

Trim: Stucco, wood, fiber cement board, composition board, or polymer millwork for built-up sections. Historic reproductions of polymer are also permitted.

Columns: Historic reproductions of wood, polymer, or fiberglass with classical entasis and proportions.

Railings: Wood milled top and bottom rails with straight or turned balusters.

Soffits and Porch Ceiling: Smooth surface composition board, plaster, T&G wood, stucco, or polymer historic reproductions.

Gutters: Ogee or half-round primed or prefinished metal. PVC is also acceptable in a color that matches trim.

Downspouts: Rectangular or round primed or prefinished metal. PVC is also permitted in a color that matches trim.

Shutters: Historic wood, polymer, or fiberglass reproductions mounted as if operable.

Foundations: Concrete, brick, or stone veneer.

Chimneys: Stucco, brick, or stone.

Front Yard Fences: Wood, prefinished metal, stone, or masonry with stucco finish.

Rear Yard Fences: Wood, prefinished metal, or masonry with stucco finish.

Colors

Siding, Windows, and Trim: White; other colors to be selected from the Liberty Color Palette.

Roof Shingles: Typically black or dark gray.

Gutters and Downspouts: Match trim color.

Shutters: Black, dark green, or a color selected from the Liberty Color Palette.

Fencing: Wood is to be white; metal is to be black or dark green.

© 1999 URBAN DESIGN ASSOCIATES

Liberty Classic

ARCHITECTURAL PATTERNS

C 7

143

Landscape Patterns

The Landscape Pattern section defines the appropriate plant and landscape palette for the private buildings and lots. The section includes discussions of: Landscape Traditions and Precedents; General Principles; Typical Lot Layouts by lot type including fencing, walls, and paving materials; Landscape Palettes by architectural style; and the Plant Palette and Matrix.

When appropriate, this section may also include lighting specifications and, for commercial pattern books, will often also include style guidelines or specifications for amenities for public spaces (e.g., benches, waste receptacles, bike racks, etc.).

Appendix

As needed, the Appendix may include excerpts from relevant building codes, developer guidelines and requirements, etc.

Sample Landscape Patterns page from the Liberty Pattern Book

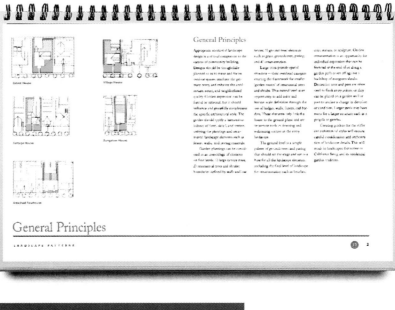

The process for creating a pattern book has several phases:

→ **Phase One**:   Understanding the Context—Past and Present
→ **Phase Two**:   Developing the Palette—Documenting Characteristics
→ **Phase Three**: Defining the Patterns—Community, Architecture, and Landscape
→ **Phase Four**: Production—Producing the Pattern Book

We work closely with a graphic design consultant who has established a format to help our in-house publications team lay out the pattern book, edit the text, and get the final product to press. The typical process takes about six months. Let's take a look at each phase more closely.

PHASE ONE: UNDERSTANDING THE CONTEXT
Past and Present

UDA Pattern Books grow out of an understanding of the regional character of a place. Thus, the design process begins by researching traditional towns in the region surrounding the project, including the houses that create their public spaces. We pay close attention to the precedents that our clients and the urban design teams have used to develop an image and character for the proposed master plan. Since UDA may sometimes be engaged to develop a pattern book for a project that was designed by other firms, it is important that we be diligent in our information-gathering efforts.

Our first meeting is with the client and the development/design team on site to understand the design, the precedents, the market, the phasing, and the process for building. This is typically a two- to three-day visit where we go out with our clients to document area precedents. We note dominant building types, architectural styles, and materials. We pay careful attention to what is fundamental to the overall fabric of the area—its prevailing style(s)—as well as to the more exotic styles that add spice to various neighborhoods. To understand local community patterns, we measure and photograph street cross sections, house setbacks, and landscape character.

We take care to photograph and document actual house types, identifying their architectural style and key details. When necessary, we engage specialists in particular architectural styles to provide us with detailed design criteria. For the Liberty Pattern Book, for example, the pattern book design team researched the tools and methods used to build the towns and neighborhoods that served as precedents for Liberty, a new town in California. The team visited ten towns, photographing and documenting house types and architectural styles. From an initial inventory of twelve potential architectural styles, six were identified as styles for the first phase of development of Liberty: Classic (California adaptations of Colonial Revival); Victorian; Arts & Crafts; European Country; Monterey Ranch; and Spanish Revival. Specialists in those styles were commissioned to provide us with detailed design criteria.

We draw the dimensions and qualities of individual neighborhood streets and public spaces in a series of cross sections that show the relationships between house facades and street space.

We also collect Sanborn Maps™ of historic settlements, city maps of precedent neighborhoods, plans for the site itself, market information about the building program, size of units, etc. This gives us a starting point from which to develop an understanding and appreciation for the context of the project.

At the same time, we may work with standard plans from a number of developers to understand the forms with which they work and to learn the qualities that they feel are important for successful marketing. This way the developer/builder's input is part of the process. This helps re-establish the collaboration between architects and builders that once existed. We then return to the office to begin sorting out what the palette might be.

PHASE TWO: DEVELOPING THE PALETTE
Documenting Characteristics

Phase Two begins with cataloguing the documented neighborhoods in photo binders. Prints and slides are sorted by place. We prepare figure-ground drawings of the precedent neighborhoods and key them to cross sections of streets and park spaces with building setbacks. We can then begin to develop building typology images based on the development program and the historic character of appropriate buildings.

At this point, we develop a first draft of an architectural palette. This includes preparing precedent boards for building types and for architectural styles using photographs and cross-section drawings as well as neighborhood plans collected as community precedents. We use these in a second working session with the development team to test the palette and its applicability to the proposed community. We prepare axonometric drawings as input to the model makers and begin developing massing drawings for each style. In articulating massing for each style, we can begin to see how the community patterns and the architectural patterns are coming together, and where we may need to work on refining our ideas still further.

Once we reach consensus with the development team on the palette, we then go through another round of more focused documentation for architectural style characteristics. The team returns to photograph details and architectural elements within each of the designated styles. These include:

→ Front elevations for door and window compositions

→ Cornices and eaves

→ Window and door types and placement

→ Porch types and details

→ Massing and materials

Liberty Precedent Photos

Classic

European Country

Arts & Crafts

Monterey Ranch

Victorian

Spanish Revival

Liberty Classic

Liberty European Country

Liberty Arts & Crafts

Liberty Monterey Ranch

Liberty Victorian

Liberty Spanish Revival

At this point, we are ready to draft the architectural palette that will be displayed at the three-day on-site model charrette that takes place during Phase Three of a pattern book project.

Note: At this stage of the project, it is useful for the project manager, in conjunction with the team, to determine the types of drawings that will be used for each category and the specific drawing specifications to be employed, e.g., scale, view, drawing type and style, etc. By establishing this as a project standard at this stage of development, we ensure consistency among all participants in the project—including other contributors such as landscape architects, perspectivist, etc. Furthermore, we save ourselves some unnecessary rework when we're ready to produce the book (or some unfortunate—and avoidable—discontinuities in drawings in the final product because time or budget precluded redoing them).

PHASE THREE: DEFINING THE PATTERNS
Community, Architecture, and Landscape

The team prepares a page-by-page outline of the book in much the same way as was described in Chapter 4 for the final report in an urban design assignment. We then create a 1" to 20' scale base map of the site plan and 1" to 20' scale wooden models of each prototype house in each category.

We set the model up in-house and the entire team reviews it together, noting any weaknesses and correcting those that are within our purview to correct before we take the model on site.

The base map and scale models are then taken to the community and used to test the plan during a three-day on-site model charrette. In addition, we draw perspective images of key addresses and, during the charrette, work toward achieving consensus regarding the desired image, lot patterns, and building mix.

Modeling Charrette

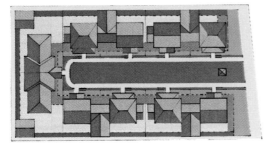

Top left:

Historic examples of Court homes include the English courts found in Pasadena and the Spanish courts and lanes found in towns like Corona del Mar.

Top right:

Character sketch of Court homes in the Liberty European Country style.

Left:

Court house arrangements as seen in this lot diagram will take many forms depending on the size and shape of the lot and the housing design. Where possible, arrangements should take advantage of axial relationships set up by adjacent streets or public spaces.

The charrette is extraordinarily revealing to our clients because it is usually the first time they will have seen a three-dimensional version of their master plan. Because the model exposes weaknesses in the master plan, we often make refinements during the model charrette. We review the community patterns, architectural patterns, and landscape patterns. We assess and adjust setbacks; lotting; specific design criteria by lot type, such as a tower on a corner house; street alignments; landscape details; parks, monuments, and open space ideas; and so forth. This is a very labor-intensive process as we go through the plan, lot by lot, documenting any changes made directly on the base map. This documentation becomes the source material for descriptions of each of the specific addresses in the Community Patterns section of the pattern book.

PHASE FOUR: PRODUCTION

Producing the Pattern Book

If for some reason it was not done previously, the first thing we must do at this point is to create a story board for the entire pattern book, page by page, identifying which drawings will be required and where they will be used. This is usually done by the project manager, in consultation with the principal-in-charge.

At the same time, final decisions should be made about which photographs and drawings will be used. Each pattern book mixes freehand drawings and hardline drawings. The type of drawings and the scale for different details should be established now, at the very beginning of the production of the draft pattern book and communicated to the entire team (including external contributors to the pattern book) before work commences on the drawings.

Pattern book teams should work closely with the graphic designer and print production personnel to set up the document within the firm's prescribed parameters for pattern book layout and drawing and text specification standards.

Now it's time to begin producing the book. Based on the feedback we've received during the charrette, the team develops a full draft of the pattern book for review by the client.

Once the draft has been developed and reviewed in-house, including a thorough proofreading, it is sent to the client for comment and, often, to builders and architects to test it out before the final version is produced.

Final production of UDA Pattern Books follows much the same overall procedure described in Chapter 4 for producing the final report for an urban design project.

Left:

Built houses along Eli's Way.

Top left:

Proposed Eli's Way in Baxter, South Carolina. Streets in Baxter will be lined with houses of different styles and varied setbacks.

Top right:

Pattern book page for Eli's Way, which will have a mix of lots ranging from 45 feet wide to 70 feet wide to accommodate a mix of different house sizes. These houses are also production builder houses and create much of the neighborhood fabric in Baxter.

TRADITIONAL ARCHITECTURE

In the course of our 35-year history, UDA has progressed forward from "modernist" to "traditional" architecture. Reconnecting architecture with its 2,000-year history enables us to build with the certainty of lessons learned by previous generations.

This means rejecting the modernist assertion that every act of building must be a completely original and personal invention. While this is a radical position to take at the beginning of the 21st century, it's a compelling one nevertheless because the concept of complete originality denies context and, therefore, is fundamentally anti-urban.

Users of architecture have never accepted our profession's abandoning of tradition. As a result, building designs that are most directly connected to the market are usually a compromise with "popular taste." Because the most talented and serious architects refused to provide traditional architecture, the building industry developed efficient techniques for mass-producing houses and shopping centers without the benefit of the best architectural talent. The result has been a divide between architecture and building. A worthwhile goal is to re-establish architecture as a source of leadership.

Finally, our culture is deeply rooted in the forms of traditional architecture. A shared vocabulary makes communication with the general public, with builders and realtors, and with the power structure of our cities and regions much easier.

By reconnecting with tradition, we can learn how to invent new forms for this new century.

The UDA Architectural Design Process: Three Phases

Cities are composed of streets, boulevards, squares and parks, buildings — all of which give form and structure to the city's public spaces. Each city has its own unique image and tradition, expressed through the character of those public spaces.

UDA works at many scales, thoughtfully designing public spaces — their facades, profiles, and floors — to build on the unique local character and the best qualities of the forms and styles inherent in that geographic region. Our architecture for individual buildings creates public spaces and a sense of community identity.

Our architectural work grows out of our urban design projects. We concentrate on developing design images for key civic or landmark buildings as well as for residential buildings that set the character and image for the development. While UDA sets the design character for these buildings, we work with local architects to complete the technical construction documents.

Another important focus of our architectural work is the development of UDA Pattern Book Houses, a portfolio of house plans for detached and attached houses that cover a broad range of the market from the most affordable houses to those that are designed for buyers with greater discretionary incomes. This portfolio can be modified to work with regional architectural patterns and is part of our comprehensive service available to developers or communities who

Architectural Styles

Colonial Revival

Classical

Victorian

Coastal

Italianate

Arts & Crafts

Mediterranean

want a seamless transition from the urban design vision to the built environment. The process we describe in this chapter refers to our residential architectural design practice. Although the local architectural firm produces the construction documents and administers the construction phase, we review the construction documents produced by associate firms and visit the site during construction to protect the integrity of the design for our clients.

Typically, we design via traditional hand drawing, although we do use computer-aided drafting to catalogue and store standard details and to produce three-dimensional bases for hand-drawn perspective drawings. By focusing our creative energies in this way, we strive to restore the architect's historical role in establishing the visual form of buildings in urban space and to use our design talents where they add the most value for our clients.

UDA's architectural practice is most frequently (but not exclusively) an extension and refinement of the drawings we create during the urban design process. For example, our facade drawings are refinements of the building images we have developed in perspective as the desired character of streets, parks, and squares emerges during the urban design process. Our wall sections are refinements of the street cross sections that delineate precisely the relationship between public and private space and define the profile of the public realm. Our floor plans are conceived to strengthen the relationship between public space and private activity.

True urbanism, however, requires many different architects and builders to provide the diversity of a town or city. Therefore, our interest in designing specific buildings is to set standards and to begin the process of city-building.

UDA'S ARCHITECTURAL PHILOSOPHY

UDA's work draws on the local architectural qualities and vocabularies of each place we work. We do this because we are committed to preserving and enhancing the local flavor these styles provide. The result is that UDA-designed buildings are unique and specific to the places in which they are located.

To achieve this, we study regional historical precedents, thoroughly researching the region's traditional building types and architectural styles to determine what is appropriate for new buildings before we begin the design process. Thus, all UDA-designed buildings are regional interpretations of traditional architectural styles. Post-modern and personal vocabularies are not practiced by UDA.

Of course, we make the buildings suitable for contemporary living. It is no small challenge to make traditional building designs respond to new patterns of living and the escalation of technology in our homes. We accommodate all the modern amenities in the designs we create, but we seek to do that in ways that do not conflict with the character and integrity of the particular style employed. Further, we pay close attention to correct building materials and methods of construction so that we can incorporate them successfully into our design recommendations and specifications.

While not limited to the styles shown, UDA most frequently draws upon the following for its building designs:

→   Colonial Revival

→   Classical

→   Victorian

→   Coastal

→   Italianate

→   Arts & Crafts

→   Mediterranean

**Examples of
UDA Architecture**

Baxter Clubhouse
Fort Hill, South Carolina

The Ledges Perspective
Huntsville, Alabama

UCI Townhouses
Cleveland, Ohio

Park DuValle House
Louisville, Kentucky

Baxter Victorian Classic
Fort Hill, South Carolina

Baxter Health Campus
Fort Hill, South Carolina

Thiel College HMC
Greenville, Pennsylvania

UDA'S ARCHITECTURAL DESIGN PRODUCTS

UDA's architectural design products fall into four primary categories and, within each category, UDA offers a varying scope of services:

→ UDA Pattern Book Houses (single-family, duplex, and townhouses)

  → Plans, elevations, front wall sections, key details

  → Builder set (by consulting architect)

  → Framing plan (by structural engineer)

  → Perspective and marketing plans

→ Custom Builder Houses for Specific Clients

  → Plans, elevations, front wall sections (other details as determined by UDA and builder)

  → Perspective and marketing plans

→ Mixed-Use Buildings, Apartment Houses, Office Buildings, Retail Buildings, and Civic Buildings

  → Plans, elevations, front wall sections (schematic design and partial design development)

  → Construction documents (via subconsultants)

UDA'S APPROACH TO ASSEMBLING AN ARCHITECTURAL DESIGN TEAM

To provide our clients with full-service architectural design capabilities, UDA takes a team approach, partnering with other firms and independent consultants whose expertise complements our own. Depending on the specific project, these may include:

Architects and Draftsmen

→ Architects who specialize in unique building types

→ Architects skilled in construction documentation and administration

→ Landscape architects

→ Home design drafting services

Engineers

→ Structural design and engineering

→ HVAC

→ Mechanical

→ Electrical

→ Lighting

→ Civil

→ Parking

Throughout the design process, we also work closely with builders and contractors, tailoring our documentation to facilitate construction.

THE UDA PROCESS FOR CREATING ARCHITECTURAL DESIGNS

As you've read in previous chapters, UDA finds a phased approach to be advantageous in working with clients. This is as true for our architectural design services as it is in the other areas of our practice, so it should come as no surprise that, while the specific content of the work is different, the phases are similar:

→ **Phase One:** Understanding the Context — Reviewing and Gathering

→ **Phase Two:** Exploring — Trying Out Ideas, Exploring Possibilities

→ **Phase Three:** Developing the Design — Final Design and Production

These three phases represent the pre-design, schematic design, and design development phases of a typical architectural project. Let's look at each phase more closely.

The love you liberate in your work is the love you keep.

ELBERT HUBBARD

Hubbard (1870 – 1911) was the founder of the Roycroft Arts and Crafts Guild and a competitor of Gustav Stickley. This quote is carved on the entrance door to the Roycroft Inn in East Aurora, New York.

PHASE ONE: UNDERSTANDING THE CONTEXT
Reviewing and Gathering

Phase One, Understanding the Context, typically entails two steps:

→ Pre-Trip Preparation
  → Review Urban Design Analysis
  → Review Master Plan Principles (and Pattern Book if available)
  → Review Building Prototypes
  → Review Market Study
  → Reach Agreement with Client Regarding Copyright Ownership
→ Trip One
  → Meeting with the Client
  → Data-Gathering

Pre-Trip Preparation

Before a glimmer of an architectural concept ever starts to form in our imaginations for a specific locale, we've got homework to do. Our first step is to review the urban design analysis, master principles, any existing building prototypes, and the pattern book if one was created. In addition, it's important that we understand the demographics and market dynamics of the area. Consequently, the architectural design team should also review any market studies germane to the project and its environs.

If UDA prepared any or all of these for our client, then clearly we have a running start on the architectural design process. If not, we should request these documents from our client and carefully and thoroughly review and discuss them in-house before we meet with our client during Trip One. Depending on how recently the materials were prepared, we should also confirm with our client that none of the assumptions, objectives, or recommendations contained in those materials have changed since the documents were created.

For illustrative purposes, this chapter will draw its examples from The Ledges, a new neighborhood in Huntsville, Alabama. UDA was selected to provide full-service architectural design for one of the homebuilders for this project. Our finished products include house designs, perspective drawings, typical floor plans, and marketing materials, including the design of the marketing brochure for the development.

In order to ensure a cohesive character to the neighborhood, the developer was committed to having houses built there that would fulfill the overall vision for the town rather than simply the individual vision of each architect engaged to design a home for a client. The builder also wanted tools that would reconnect architecture to the homebuilding industry. To do so, the developer understood that it needed design direction to provide to architects — direction regarding critical components such as massing, overall floor plan, image, and key details.

UDA created the pattern book for The Ledges. As part of the process, we researched precedent house styles in both Twickenham and Mooresville, in the Huntsville area, and had those concepts as a platform for further development. We also conducted an analysis that focused on the overall plan of the subdivision, its park spaces, and the relationship of the houses to public space and available views. For example, our urban design sensibilities led us to incorporate features — such as full front porches — as key components of the design concepts for the houses in this development.

Part of our job is to ensure that the architectural designs are consistent with marketplace parameters. For The Ledges, the market study indicated that houses in the 3,000- to 3,500-square-foot range would be the most marketable. The general area is home to a rather highly educated population, both families and "empty nesters." The floor plans take these lifestyle factors into consideration in space allocation, space utilization relationships, and room configurations.

Design Criteria and Program Requirements — The Ledges

Square Footage

| 2 of 4 | 2800–3000 sq. ft. Master up |
| 2 of 4 | 3000–3300 sq. ft. Master down |

Minimum Room Sizes

Study	12' x 12'
Dining	12' x 14' or 13' x 13'
Master BR	13' x 16' 6"
Master Bath	8' x 12'
Great Room	14' x 18'
Smallest BR	11' x 12'

Design plans w/4 BR or 3 BR w/bonus room, 3½ bath; one bath up

Plan for accessibility and visitability. See Appendix E.

Another important factor that should be addressed up front on an architectural design project is the matter of who retains the rights to the design. Unless otherwise negotiated with the client (and such instances would be rare), UDA retains the copyright on the designs, and a copyright notice should be placed on each design document.

Trip One

Trip One provides us with an opportunity to accomplish a variety of planning and information-gathering tasks, as well as finalizing the building program with our client before we begin exploring architectural design solutions in detail.

Planning Tasks. Planning tasks typically include:

→ Review of the overall design process, scope of work, and schedule

→ Review of the agenda for Trip One

→ Assessment of the adequacy of the hard data accumulated to date to determine what other hard data need to be acquired (e.g., zoning regulations, building codes, topographic maps, etc.)

→ Development and/or review of the building program and budget including the general plan requirements (note below the General Plan Requirements developed for The Ledges)

→ Review of the preferred construction methods and materials (Refer to the Materials and Methods of Construction Checklist shown on page 162. We use this to solicit input from the developer and/or builder. The responses provided are those that were obtained from the contractor for The Ledges.)

Data-Gathering Tasks. Typically the client has some hard data for us as a starting point. We often have participated in the development of these — a master plan, a pattern book, a perspective drawing of the urban space, and a diagrammatic plan of the district. We may also want to do photo reconnaissance, although, if we have created a pattern book for the site, we may already have the necessary source material in our files. If not, we'll want to do the photo reconnaissance during Trip One.

Other hard data to collect during Trip One include:

→ A site survey

→ All pertinent topographic information

→ Information regarding utilities

→ Zoning

→ Historic surveys

→ Applicable building codes/accessibility requirements

→ Existing building plans the contractor may want to use as a basis
   for the new designs

In the case of The Ledges, the builder had existing plans it wanted to adapt. During Trip One it was decided that we would develop three of the four house models from their existing plans. We were asked to address the basic location of rooms and the overall massing, and to develop house designs using architectural vocabularies that supported the image of the site and were based on area precedents.

We discussed the contractor's preferred method of construction — in this case, long spans with engineered floor joists and crawl space foundations — so that we could develop appropriate design solutions.

During Trip One, it is also important to reach agreement with the client concerning the specific products to be produced and the timetable for the delivery of those materials. For The Ledges, the specific products UDA was engaged to produce consisted of:

→ Floor plans and foundation plan

→ Elevations

→ Framing plans

→ Key exterior details

→ Elevations of key interior walls

→ Electrical plans

Materials and Methods of Construction Checklist

Element	Question/Assumptions	Answer/Comments
Foundations	Raised slab construction typical, some units to have basement	Options
	Poured-in-place concrete foundation walls, 10"?	Yes
	Brick veneer above grade?	Yes
	Do you have a typical wall section detail we could reference?	Yes
Exterior Walls	2 x 6 wood studs; panelized; blown insulation	
Floors	Concrete slab first floor	Locate all slab plumbing
	Open web wood joists at second floor	
	First floor ceiling height: 10'; (11'—Italianate)	12" floor structure
	Second floor ceiling height: 9'; (10'—Italianate)	12" floor structure
Roof	Stick framed	
	Composition shingles, metal (5V-Crimp) and synthetic slate	
	What do you prefer to use for porch roofs less than 3:12 slope?	Metal
	Continuous ridge vent with composition shingles; with others?	Gable vents
Cladding & Trim	Siding: wood (cypress?) fiber-cement?	Fiber cement—5" reveal
	Wood or composite moldings?	Wood
	Wood or engineered wood trim?	MDF base and crown
	Soffit material? Continuous soffit vent?	Fiber cement, yes
	Modular size brick/Do you ever use oversize (2 1/4" h)?	Only when using salvage brick
Windows	Weather Shield, double-hung, w/simulated divided lights	
	Wood or clad?	Wood
	Entry doors: Do you have a preferred product?	Shop-made wood
Porches & Stoops	Concrete slab at first floor; decking at second floor	
	(tongue-and-groove wood?)	Yes
	Brick, cast stone, or stone steps?	Brick
	Wood railings; iron rails?	Wood
	Wood or composite columns?	Composite
Chimneys	Brick, stucco	

Finalizing the Building Program. If a master plan and a pattern book already exist, we will confirm the desired architectural imagery and stylistic vocabulary for the project and finalize the building program during Trip One. Typically, the program is described in the form of a rough sketch — an "esquisse." In addition to setting the architectural imagery and stylistic vocabulary, the esquisse reconciles the client program with the massing of prototype building(s) and includes conceptual floor plans and elevation diagrams. These hand-drawn sketches are key to establishing the design direction for the project.

If a master plan and a pattern book are not available, then we would first need to do the research to gain the necessary understanding of the context. In that case, the esquisse would not be done until Phase Two — Exploring. Since UDA had previously created The Ledges Pattern Book, we were able to produce an esquisse for that project during Trip One and advance to Phase Two: Exploring.

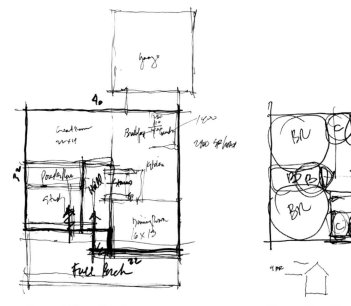

Ground Floor Esquisse   **Upper Floor Esquisse**

PHASE TWO:
EXPLORING THE POSSIBILITIES

Trying Out Ideas, Exploring Possibilities

Phase Two is the part of the architectural design process where we try out ideas, investigate options, and explore alternatives.

Phase Two consists of three parts:

→ Development of handcrafted schematic floor plans, elevations, and a wall section

→ An in-house charrette

→ Defining the marketing materials required

Note: At this stage of the project, it is useful for the project manager, in conjunction with the team, to determine the specific types of drawings that will be developed for the final design package. UDA has a standard list of drawings that we use as a punchlist for confirming the specific drawings to be produced for a particular project. In addition, UDA has developed specifications for drawings — marker colors, line weights, proportion, scale, etc. — to ensure consistency in overall approach and design values regardless of the specific design content. This adds a tangible level of sophistication and polish to the appearance of our finished products and, not incidentally, eliminates a number of avoidable technical hassles for our consultants, graphic designer, and printing vendors. Furthermore, we save ourselves some unnecessary rework when we're ready to produce the final design package if everyone works with the same set of drawing standards throughout the process.

Drawing Techniques and Scales

To ensure technical consistency among our architectural drawings, UDA has adopted the following techniques and scales for the types of drawings we customarily provide for architectural projects:

Techniques:

Hardline drawings — Use pencil on tracing paper.

Freehand sketching — Do in ink over the hardline drawings to explore alternatives.

Renderings — Use colored pencils, markers, or watercolors.

Perspectives — Use line weight of pencils to shade and shadow; vary the line weight to articulate the design intent.

Typical Drawing Set and Scales:

Some of these drawings are developed in preliminary form during the esquisse that occurs in Phase One or as part of an existing pattern book. They are then refined during Phase Two and finalized during Phase Three. While the design details evolve during that process, the scales are to remain consistent.

Site Plan: 1:20

Floor Plans: $1/8$" = 1'

Elevations : $1/8$" = 1'

Roof Plan: $1/8$" = 1'

Front Wall Section: $3/4$" = 1'

Key Details: $11/2$" = 1'

Standard Windows and Doors: $3/4$" = 1'

Interior Elevations: $3/8$" = 1'

Building Sections: $3/8$" = 1'

Developing Handcrafted Schematic Floor Plans and Elevations

From the information gathered during Trip One and the esquisse, the team can now begin producing schematic floor plans and elevations. For The Ledges, illustrations were created for four house types. Two of the house types are illustrated in two different architectural styles on the following spread.

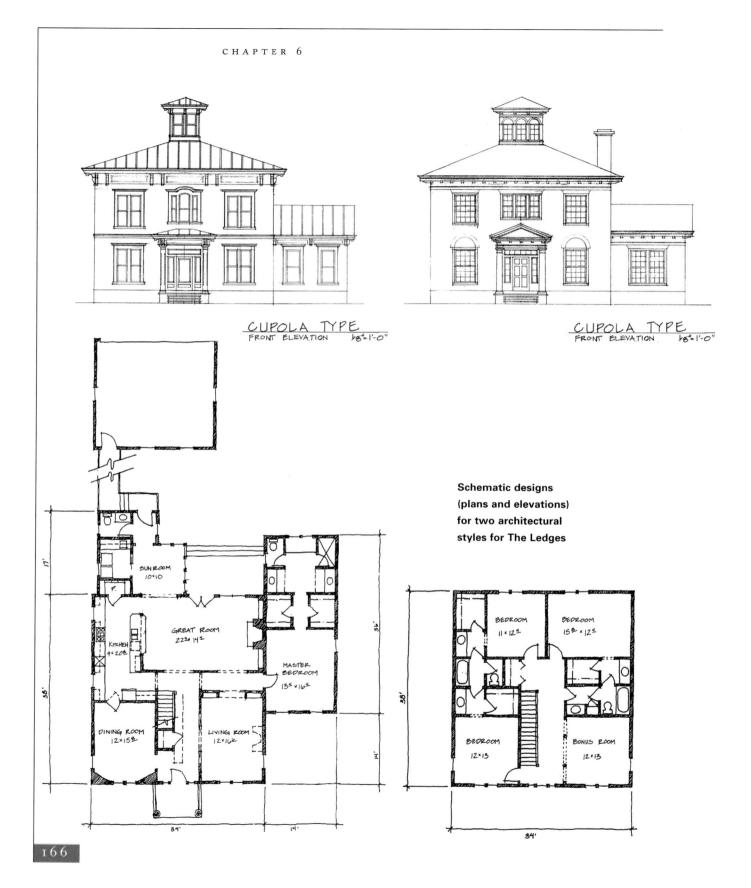

CUPOLA TYPE
FRONT ELEVATION   ⅛"=1'-0"

CUPOLA TYPE
FRONT ELEVATION   ⅛"=1'-0"

**Schematic designs
(plans and elevations)
for two architectural
styles for The Ledges**

SUN ROOM
10×10

GREAT ROOM
22¾×14¾

KITCHEN
9×20⅛

MASTER
BEDROOM
13¾×16¾

DINING ROOM
12×15⅛

LIVING ROOM
12×16⅛

BEDROOM
11×12¾

BEDROOM
15⅛×12¾

BEDROOM
12×13

BONUS ROOM
12×13

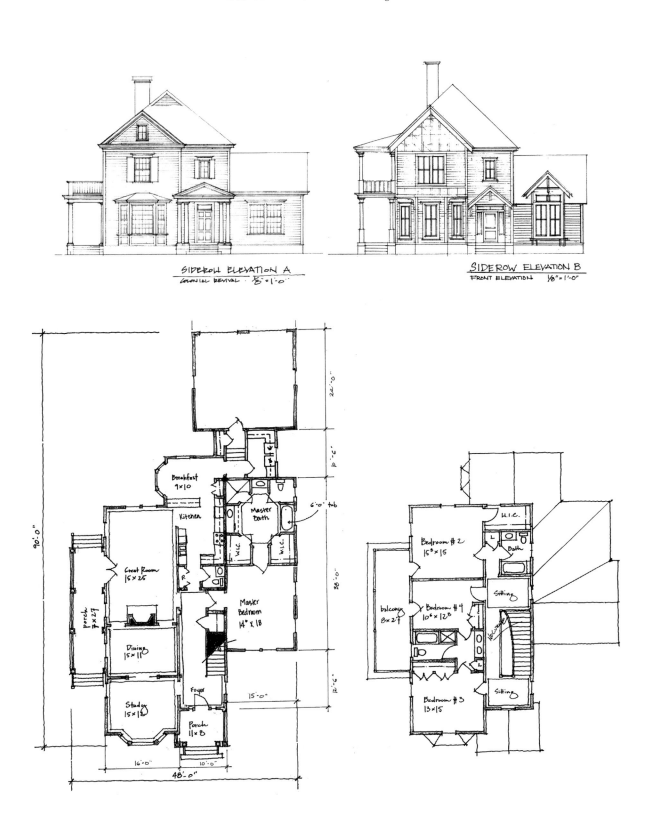

SIDEROLL ELEVATION A
COLONIAL REVIVAL ⅛" = 1'-0"

SIDEROW ELEVATION B
FRONT ELEVATION ⅛" = 1'-0"

windows @ first & second floor
are 2'-8" x 6'-6" (2 over 2
divided light pattern), typical.

12
12

6" chamfered
square columns

2'-0"

1'-0"

7'-1¼"

6'-6"

9'-2"

7'-1"

1'-9"

10'-1¼"

6'-6"

see detail on
other sheet

* mirror on opp. side

2'-8"

1st floor head height: 0'-0"
2nd floor head height: 0'-0"

¼" = 1'-0"
22 Nov 99

Working elevation

Presentation elevation

Producing the Drawings

We produce both line drawings and rendered line drawings to illustrate the architectural designs we create for clients. These drawings may be developed during an in-house work session—or they may be created in the context of a charrette. In either case, it is important that we keep in mind the programmatic objectives of the developer vis-à-vis the floor plans (paying particular attention to room size and room relationships) and elevation options we've developed. We spend considerable time and effort looking at a lot of precedents—not just from the field-gathering we have done, but also from books and archival photographs. This process of relating the concepts we develop to historical precedents continues to the end of the project.

As shown on pages 166 and 167, for The Ledges, each house had two styles applied to each plan.

Reviewing and Revising the Drawings

Next, we review the preliminary drawings with our client—either at the close of the work session or during the charrette. We refine the overall designs and available options for each house based on the results of this review. Feature by feature, we work with the client to assess the individual designs. Are bay windows appropriate? Should there be an option for a two-story porch? We continue in this manner until we have worked through the process for each basic house design.

As part of this process, we also coordinate the floor plans and elevations, adjusting them, as necessary, to be compatible.

Defining the Marketing Materials Required

Once the in-house work session is completed, it's time to hold a working session with our client to review the overall designs, identify the various design options that should be included, and verify the scope and form of the final product. The local real estate community is often involved in the process. We can assist the client in introducing real estate brokers to the product, familiarizing them with

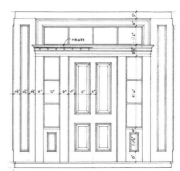

Elevation detail

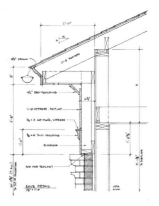

Eave detail

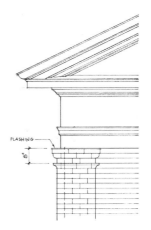

Cornice detail

key features and benefits. We can also obtain their input regarding the market receptivity they anticipate to the designs, floor plans, and amenities, and any suggestions they have for architectural modifications or refinements that would enhance the marketability of the location.

After discussing these ideas, we verify with our client what the final product will entail, including any options they wish to make available to homebuyers, and develop a detailed checklist of the drawings and other materials to be included in the final design package.

For The Ledges, the checklist of drawings and materials for the final design package (builder's set) contains:

→ Foundation Plan
→ Floor Plans
→ Roof Plan
→ Framing Plans
→ Elevations (4)
→ Building Sections (2)
→ Wall Section
→ Interior Elevations (1–2)
→ Eave and Cornice Details
→ Detail Elevations of Front Door and Typical Window
→ Window and Door Details and Schedules
→ Electrical Plans

Sample pages from a builder's set are shown on pages 173 and 174.
We're now ready to move on to Phase Three.

PHASE THREE: DEVELOPING THE DESIGN

Final Design and Production

Phase Three contains two major steps:

→ Completing the materials to be included in the final design package

→ Coordinating in-house and vendor production of the design package

Completing the Materials to be Included in the Final Design Package

At this point in the process, the team needs to:

→ Assess the existing drawings and undertake any additional work required to bring them to final, publishable form

→ Identify and create any additional drawings that are required (e.g., digital floor plans, elevations, wall sections, key details, etc.)

→ Create eye-level perspectives (below)

→ Provide consultants (local architects and engineers) with specifications for the drawings they will provide (e.g., preferred type of digital file; scale; orientation — i.e., horizontal or vertical; typography specifications for drawing labels, etc.)

→ Transform the sketches into hardline drawings, as appropriate

→ Create a perspective rendering (see page 171) and floor plans (see pages 173 and 174) for marketing purposes

→ Make sure that UDA copyright notice appears on all drawings created by UDA, regardless of the form these materials take (hard copy or electronic)

→ Work with the development team to name and describe the house style(s) (e.g., lineage, main amenities, basic information such as room types and square footage, etc.)

The perspective rendering and the marketing floor plans provide the final graphic visualization of the design and are the heart of the marketing brochure. In most cases, we work with our graphic design consultant to create an image for the marketing materials. Text for the brochure will be supplied by the development team and incorporated into the layout for the brochure. When needed or desirable, UDA can offer the client copywriting and editing services to support the development of these marketing materials.

Final Design Package (Builder's Set)

At this stage of the project, we pay particular attention to the materials and products that will become part of the construction specifications for each building or type of building at the site. UDA details the materials of construction, carefully identifying material and product options that will realize the design in three-dimensional form. These specifications are sent to the client for review. When we have obtained approval on these from our client, the outline specifications are given to the drafting service or local or associated architecture firm that will produce the construction drawings. UDA reviews these drawings, typically when they are 50% complete. It is not unusual at this stage to identify additional sketches that are required for clarification. Once reviewed and any new drawings created, these materials go back to the draftsman or architect for completion. UDA reviews the final drawings before they are released to the client.

These drawings are finalized in Phase Three, building on the work completed during Phase Two and reflecting our further exploration of material and product options that will realize the design in three-dimensional form.

Sample pages from Builder's Set

Sample pages from Builder's Set

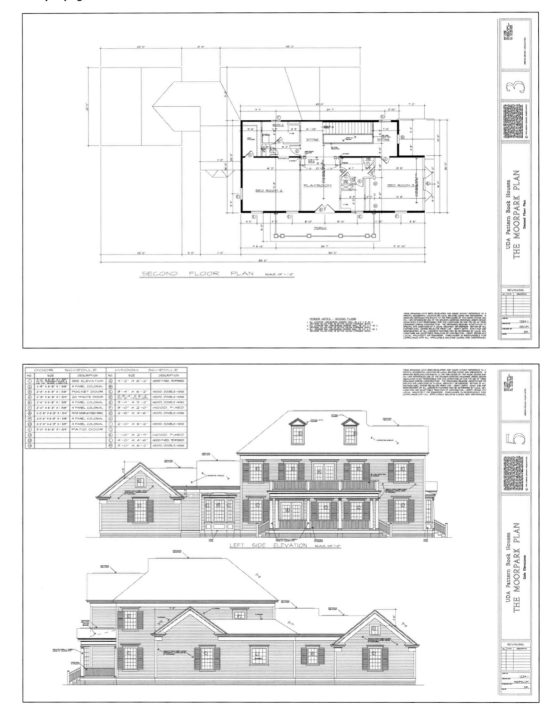

Coordinating In-House and Vendor Production of the Marketing Brochure/Materials

To produce the final design package, the project team needs to coordinate with the in-house publishing team.

The publications manager should be given a completed checklist of all materials to be contained in the final design package, including information about the intended production method and quantities required. Some materials are produced in-house at UDA and spiral-bound. Some may go to commercial printers. The project manager and the publications manager determine what is most appropriate for the project given the client's needs, the deliverable quantities included in the contract, the publication budget, and the delivery date.

Team members coordinate with any outside consultants to ensure that their materials will be submitted on a timely basis.

All drawings will need to be reviewed, redlined, and revised one last time before they are released for final production. Team members are expected to refer to UDA's *Graphic Guidelines for Marketing Publications* (see Appendix D) and to consult with the project and publications managers for any other stylistic or formatting conventions that are specific to a particular project.

Remember that the quality of these finished materials is essential to the client's success in marketing the development, and that these materials are extremely valuable marketing tools for the firm.

Samples of UDA's marketing materials for The Ledges are shown on pages 176 and 177.

Eufala Italianate

Eufala Colonial Revival

2-Car Garage

Breakfast Room

Kitchen

Great Room

Master Bedroom

Dining Room

Study

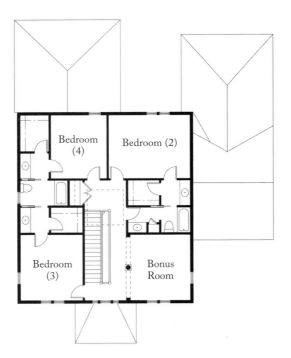

Bedroom (4)

Bedroom (2)

Bedroom (3)

Bonus Room

Floor Plans and Elevations for Marketing Materials

**Sample pages from
The Ledges of Huntsville Mountain
Marketing brochure and insert
sheets designed by Wolfe Design**

UDA is justifiably proud of our computer systems and capacity to produce documents in a variety of formats with in-house color plotting and printing. Ironically, our most valued products are hand-drawn: UDA X-Rays, through which we learn by drawing the footprints of buildings and outlines of natural features; "portraits," in which the intensity of color made by hand creates a vivid interpretation of a place rather than a neutral representation; eye-level perspectives, in which the subtleties of an image could only be created by hand; complex aerial perspectives, in which the major concepts emerge clearly from the complexities of context, but are anchored in them; facades of buildings with proportions and forms carefully emphasized with line work; and lot plans of houses illustrating the potential development of "rooms" for outdoor living.

All of these gain their power from the process by which they were made. They are original works with direct connections between mind, hand, and eye. Yet we could not do these hand drawings without the computer. The hand is guided by a precise representation of reality.
Nor could we produce them without the capacity
to scan, adjust, format, and reproduce them.

In this digital age, UDA's products are sometimes thought to be anachronisms—not of this time. Yet futurists tell us that as mass production, digital production, and the Information Age proceed, handmade objects and personal attention will be the most cherished. Therefore, our products are very much "of our time."

Appendices >

UDA's Filing System — Overview and General Filing Procedures

UDA has five general categories of project-specific materials that must be labeled and filed in a manner that promotes efficient storage and quick, easy retrieval as needed. The five categories are:

→   Project files for papers and correspondence

→   Computer files for word processing, spreadsheets, CADD, and graphics

→   Flat files for drawings (labels)

→   Tube files for drawings (labels)

→   Flat box files for drawings and models (labels)

Each team has a template for labels located on its designated team space on the network server.

Of course we have other documents in files — e.g., financial, insurance, 401k, personnel — but these are maintained separately by our administrative personnel and do not need to be dealt with here.

FILE NAMES AND ORGANIZATION

Our guiding principle in file names and organization is "Keep It Simple."
The number of file divisions for any given project should be kept to a minimum.

Urban Design Projects

Each urban design project should have the following five or six subfiles:

Subfile	Title	Contents and Special Instructions
1	Correspondence	Incoming and outgoing letters, memos, faxes, and copies of e-mail
		Organize correspondence in reverse chronological order, the most recent on top
		For larger projects, subdivide correspondence by date — i.e., one or two months per file folder — as is useful
2	Transmittal Forms (Optional)	Teams may choose to maintain a separate file for all incoming and outgoing transmittals
3	Minutes / Meeting Notes	Typed minutes and handwritten or typed notes from meetings and telephone calls
4	Reports / Drawings	Interim and final drafts
		Photos and small images to be included in the reports
		For projects with more than one report, create one hanging file with separate subfiles
		File 8½" x 11" copies of *all* project drawings in this file
5	Contract / Invoicing	Original proposal, signed agreement, and subconsultant proposals and agreements
		Ongoing invoicing information and spreadsheets
6	Background Information	Marketing reports, comprehensive plans and zoning ordinances, demographic information, etc.
		For larger projects, use a separate hanging file with its own subfiles
		Store binders and other large items that do not fit in the filing cabinets on the shelves above the flat files

File Naming Conventions

All correspondence file names must end with this format:

→   Format: lastname-yrmody.wpd (or other appropriate word
                    processing file extensions)

→   Example: geisman-990726.wpd

That is, the addressee's last name, a hyphen, the date in 6 digits with
year/month/day, a period, and the file type extension. This makes it very easy
to find correspondence alphabetically and chronologically by addressee.

Thus, the string for a file name for a letter would read:

→   Format: drive:\project number\file type\addressee last name-
                    yrmody.file type extension

→   Example: L:\1162\Correspondence\geisman-990726.wpd

Files in other subfolders should also always end with the same yrmody.
file extension convention.

Using the "File" Stamp

If this is not already set up as a file macro on your computer:

→   Stamp all correspondence with the "File" stamp below the enclosure
    and cc lines on the last page

→   Stamp the front page of memos and faxes

Quattro Pro Files

→   Store project-related Quattro® Pro files within the individual project files
    on the designated drive on the server.

→   Use a numbering/naming system similar to the correspondence file naming
    convention for these files

    →   Format: drive:\project number\file type\filename-yrmody.file
                    type extension

    →   Examples: L:\1162\spreadsheet\-990611

Pattern Book Projects

Follow previous procedures for Urban Design project filing.

Architecture Projects

The filing system for Architecture projects varies somewhat depending on the complexity of the individual project. Schematic Design projects can be set up using the system outlined above for Urban Design projects.

Full-service Architecture projects, because they are more complex, should be organized as follows:

Subfile # / Title

1   General Correspondence

2   Subconsultant Correspondence

    2A   Subconsultant A

    2B   Subconsultant B

    2C   Subconsultant C

    2D   Subconsultant D

3   Transmittals In

4   Transmittals Out

5   Meeting Minutes

6   Geotechnical & Survey Information

7   Agency Approval, Building Code, Zoning

8   Field Reports

9   Bidding

10   Change Orders

11   Contractor Requests for Payment

12   Test Reports

13   Reference Materials

14   Contract

15 – 99   Project Defined Files

FILING PROCEDURES

Team Files Are the Team's Responsibility

Each project team has its own bank of filing cabinets and is responsible for maintaining its own project files. The team is also responsible for maintaining the flat surface above its files.

Interns Handle Day-to-Day File Maintenance

Each team assigns an intern or interns to maintain the team's project files.

All file drawers are labeled to identify their contents. At a minimum, the label should contain the project number(s) and name(s) of project files contained within the drawer. For projects that require multiple drawers, labels should include additional file type or time frame information to expedite filing and retrieval.

Project Managers Maintain Active Files at Their Desks

Project managers should maintain *Active Files* (i.e., files of current correspondence, spreadsheets, invoices, contract information, etc.) at their desks, either organized in baskets or in file folders. The project manager is responsible for "tagging" all documents with the file number and subfile designation (in red pen at the top right corner of the document) before placing them in the Active File baskets or folders.

Main Project Files Are Updated Weekly

Every Monday morning between 8:30 and 9:30 (during the project managers' meeting) the interns file items from the bottom/back of each Active File into Main Project Files. Flat File and photo/slide filing takes place during this time as well. Each team should decide what—and how much—to leave in the Active Files.

Files Are Archived Semi-Annually

During the first week of March and October, each team boxes stale files and sends them to our long-term archive storage facility. Digital project files are also archived onto Zip disks or CDs at this time.

B

UDA's CADD Filing System

UDA'S CADD SOFTWARE CAPABILITIES

Since most CADD software has its own inherent structure, it is important that everyone understand the way in which we use CADD files in the work we do. We currently have two different CADD software programs:

→ ARRIS

→ AutoCAD

Each has its own unique strengths, and we select the program(s) to be used based on the specific requirements of the project.

ARRIS 2001

The current release, ARRIS 2001, is a suite of tools, including drafting, architectural construction documentation and detailing, site design, 3D modeling and rendering (opaque and shade/shadow), that has been used for architectural projects. Higher-end rendering is possible through direct export to Lightscape.

→ ARRIS reads and writes AutoCAD Release V2.5, 2.6, 12 thru 14 & 2000 .DWG and industry standard .DXF files.

→ Drawings can be viewed and plotted without a license from any PC station where the software is loaded.

→ An integrated ARRISView 2D and 3D viewer tool (now sold as eZ Meeting) allows project managers to view and mark up ARRIS, .DWG, and image files without having to know CADD.

→ eZ Meeting allows the same viewing and mark-up features among project teams via the Internet.

AutoCAD 2002

Many of the files that we send to and receive from clients or consultants are in AutoCAD.DWG format. Having a copy of AutoCAD allows us to plot files without having to do any translations. We often use this software to import city base maps into our system so that the maps are available as underlays for UDA's hand-drawn x-rays. It is also important for us to check the content and accuracy of .DWG files that we export from other CADD packages before we send them on.

ARRIS is a trademark of Sigma Design International, LLC.
AutoCAD is a trademark of AutoDesk Incorporated.
Lightscape is a trademark of AutoDesk Incorporated.
eZ Meeting is a trademark of Sigma Design International, LLC.
Quattro Pro is a trademark of Corel Corporation.

FILE ORGANIZATION

The inherent project and file organization for each CADD package is different. Training sessions specific to each program will provide you with more in-depth discussion of issues not covered here.

Some CADD applications expect certain folders and files to be in a predetermined location. These conventions need to be observed in order to make files available to the entire team and to others in the studio. The design team leader and the IT specialist in the firm can direct you to the proper location for project folders on the CADD system. At UDA, the IT specialist is the Studio Architect for Technology.

When setting up project folders and filing CADD materials, UDA adheres to these standards:

→   Project folder names should contain some form of project identification, such as a project number and/or a project name. Where the CADD application's naming conventions allow a limited number of characters, the project number is preferred over the project name.

→   The preferred filing location for each software program is:

>   →   **ARRIS:** Workgroups\ARRISdbs — filed by project number (e.g., 1000.pj)

>   →   **AutoCAD:** In team's project folders

→   Project files should be stored on the server in order to assure that files are properly backed up on nightly tapes and to allow others access to the files. Do not store projects long-term on your local computer hard drive.

C

UDA's Image/Graphic and Publication Filing System

UDA has developed a system for naming, filing, and archiving computer-based image, graphic, and publication files. These procedures allow us to maintain orderly, easy, and effective storage and retrieval of these files, as well as efficient use of our network space.

Each UDA team has been assigned its own discrete and limited network storage space for its image and publication files. Each team has the responsibility for maintaining its own drive area and for creating Extensis Portfolio™ indices. Archiving is done centrally by the Studio Architect for Technology. However, the teams are responsible for preparing project files for that process.

ORGANIZATION OF THE TEAM DRIVE SPACE

To promote quick recognition and ease of access to the desired files, UDA has established this general organizational structure for team drive space:

Team Folder **(Figure 1)**

→   Each team has its own folder.

→   Folders are assigned to a specific drive on the network server.

Project Folders **(Figure 2)**

→   Teams set up these folders for each project.

→   The folder name consists of the four-digit project code followed by the project name in standard English with word space (e.g., 1308 Duluth).

We recommend that you protect these folders by inhibiting the rename and delete options.

Primary Subfolders **(Figure 3)**

→   Teams have some discretion in naming these subfolders.

→   An Images and a Publications subfolder should be present in each job folder.

Secondary Subfolders **(Figure 4)**

→   All individual files must be placed in a secondary subfolder. There should be no files stored individually outside of the secondary subfolders.

→   Each team names its own secondary subfolders, organizing its files in the way that makes the most sense for the nature of the materials.

→   For example, under the primary subfolder "Images," there may be a series of pattern book house types, or folders representing chapters in a report.

→   Under the primary subfolder "Publications," there may be a series of folders for pattern books, reports, boards, and other publication types.

Note: Do not layer folders beyond this secondary level. If additional sorting of files is necessary, create folders at the primary and secondary levels only.

Teams are required to set up all new projects using this system and to retrofit old projects as they are prepared for archiving so that all projects will ultimately conform to this system.

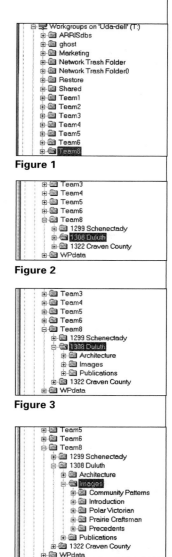

Figure 1

Figure 2

Figure 3

Figure 4

FILE NAMING CONVENTIONS

Separate file naming conventions have been established for graphic/image files and for report/publication files as follows:

Graphic/Image Files

Job/Project Number:	Four digits
Item Type:	3- to 6-letter abbreviation
Optional Info:	User defined
Iteration:	Copy, version, or sequence
File Extension:	Period (.) followed by format extension

Publication Files (QuarkXPress™ documents)

Job/Project Number:	Four digits
Item Type:	Rpt or Brd, etc.
Identifier:	Master
Iteration:	Section, copy, or version
File Extension:	Period (.) followed by format extension

Except for the period that precedes the file extensions, do not use any punctuation or special characters in the file names. Write the name in upper and lower case letters with no spaces between name components. Use an initial cap for each component abbreviation of the file name. Keep the file name as brief as possible.

INDEXING GRAPHIC/IMAGE FILES WITH PORTFOLIO

The use of Portfolio software to graphically index individual image files is an important part of each team's organizational responsibilities. Archiving and accessing depend upon consistent, current, and complete Portfolio documentation of image files. In addition, this index expedites retrieval from both the active drive and the archive disks.

Examples of Graphic File Names

1308Photo2styHouse3.tif

1308SectSpringSt.jpg

1308PerspSpringSt2.tif

Examples of Publication File Names

1308RptMasterIntro.qxd

1308PBMasterCommPatten.qxd

1308PatternBook.qxd

1308BoardPrecedents.qxd

Suggested Item Types for Graphic Files

aerial (Aerial)

perspective [eye-level] (Persp)

plan (Plan)

section (Sect)

elevation (Elev)

detail (Det)

diagram (Diag)

axo (Axo)

xray (Xray)

photograph (Photo)

Here are the steps involved in indexing graphic and image files with Portfolio:

Create a Portfolio for each project level folder. The ideal location for the Portfolio document is within the primary subfolder "Images." Unless instructed otherwise by the project team leader, this is where the Portfolio document should reside. When the number of files is unusually large, or needs to be organized into discrete groupings, you may create separate Portfolio documents in the secondary subfolders.

Create a Portfolio for all of the project images when the project is archived to CD. This comprehensive Portfolio document may be the working portfolio contained within the active job folder (as described above), or one newly created while the project is being prepared for archiving. Individual subportfolios created within secondary subfolders will be archived to the CD along with the image files, but they do not eliminate the requirement that a master portfolio be created prior to archiving.

Note: The Portfolio catalogue must be updated as new images are added or deleted.

ARCHIVING

To ensure easy retrieval of information in the future, team files must comply with the filing system. Historic or legacy file organization structures that may have been useful to project teams while the project was active must be revised to conform to our standard system prior to archiving. Projects that do not comply with these standards will not be archived.

Two Kinds of Archival CDs

When projects are archived, two kinds of archival CDs are produced: Publication CDs and Image CDs.

Publication CDs (marked with a red dot). Publication CDs usually contain one QuarkXPress (Quark) document (such as a report or precedent boards) and copies of all of the attendant images (collected for output). Large documents, such as pattern books, may be divided across multiple CDs, by chapter, when they are archived. Very small or minor Quark publications from one project may be grouped on one CD. When these CDs are accessed, all of the information for output should be present (Quark documents and attendant images).

Image CDs (marked with a blue dot). Image CDs are where *all* images associated with each project are archived, whether an image is currently used in a publication or not. The correct use of UDA's folder organizational system is most critical for these archives since the two levels of subfolders from the drive space become the organizational system for the CD. The comprehensive Portfolio document will be saved on the CD to provide a graphic index for the images contained.

Preparation for Archiving

The actual transfer of files to the CDs is handled by the publications team. They review the project folder with the team for compliance with the organizational requirements and for inclusion of a comprehensive image portfolio. Teams must be sure to schedule adequate time to complete the archiving process. "Emergency" archiving is not an option.

Archival CD Library

As archival CDs are burned, they are placed in the library. Two copies of each CD will be burned—one for circulation and one for permanent storage.

The organization of the CDs follows standard office practice and is by project number. A sign-out system tracks borrowed CDs.

Graphic Guidelines

UDA has developed comprehensive graphic guidelines for all of its marketing publications and client deliverables. Consistency in the design of our publications creates an impression of unity and structure — a perception that strengthens the impact and effectiveness of the materials we produce for our clients and for our own marketing purposes. We strongly encourage firms to develop graphic guidelines appropriate to the nature of their work for the cohesiveness these standards add to the end product.

UDA's guidelines have been published separately in a volume entitled "Graphic Guidelines for Marketing Publications." Within that document, we include graphic standards for:

A   The Basic Elements *(Grid, Typography, Color, Paper)*

B   Case Study Books

C   Deliverable Books

D   Proposals

Sample page formats for case study books, deliverable books, and proposals are included in the guidelines book. Type specifications and electronic templates are provided for the sample pages shown. When creating a new publication, all personnel refer to the Graphic Guidelines to select the electronic template that best fits the type of publication being produced.

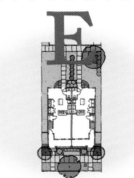

Accessibility and Visitability

Urban Design Associates is dedicated to creating environments in which a full range of living, working, and shopping experiences are accessible, both physically and psychologically. Our mixed-use neighborhoods are designed to provide a wide range of housing types to create a mixed-income urban environment that promotes social interaction and provides access to the functions of daily life without needing an automobile.

It is therefore important to make sure that all efforts are made to provide buildings and environments that are accessible to the physically disabled. There is increasing awareness that previous efforts, while successful in increasing the number of fully accessible housing units, have only dealt with part of the problem. In some ways, this program has perpetuated the isolation of disabled people into those 5% of the housing units that are fully accessible. Architectural barriers often prevent the kind of social interaction so essential to building social capital in neighborhoods by making it impossible for disabled people to visit friends and neighbors. Such barriers also prevent residents who develop disabilities from remaining in their homes, thus forcing out of the neighborhood some of the people most in need of a "pedestrian-oriented" community.

The concept of "visitability," described simply as enabling a physically disabled person to visit a house for dinner, has been developed to deal with this issue. This includes one zero-step entrance to the living level of the house, doorways wide enough to accommodate a wheelchair, and a bathroom that can be used by a person in a wheelchair. It does not call for a fully accessible bathroom with turning radii within itself, but rather simple devices such as an out-swinging door on a powder room.

Some of the physical forms of traditional neighborhood design appear, at first glance, to be at odds with these goals. For instance, front porches, an American tradition, are most effective when raised above street level and, in urban settings, houses with shallow front yards, or with row houses directly adjacent to sidewalks, have raised ground floors. This change of level is necessary to avoid having windows into the private areas of houses at eye level of pedestrians on the sidewalk, an unlivable condition that severely compromises the marketability of urban housing. The problem is, this same feature makes it difficult to make a house accessible.

The challenge is to provide both good urban form and increased access for disabled people. Multi-family buildings with elevators and single-family houses with deep front yards often can be built with a zero-step entrance from the street. For building types too close to the sidewalk to achieve this from the front, a zero-step entry can be provided in the back yard where, in any case, the parking is located. A zero-step entry can be accomplished either with a ramp or by grading the site with the rear yard at an elevation higher than the street.

While the zero-step entrance is an effective solution, there remain obstacles to achieving it, particularly in affordable and lower-cost housing. Although easily achieved with raised slab construction, it is more difficult with wood frame houses that have crawl spaces, especially those houses with pier foundations.

Uniform Federal Accessibility Standards (UFAS)–Compliant Units

1. Accessible parking spaces and curb cut
2. Accessible route to building
3. Barrier-free entrance to building
4. 32" clear opening at doors (34" doors) and clear space at doors
5. Accessible kitchen
6. Accessible bathroom
7. Barrier-free access to porches from units

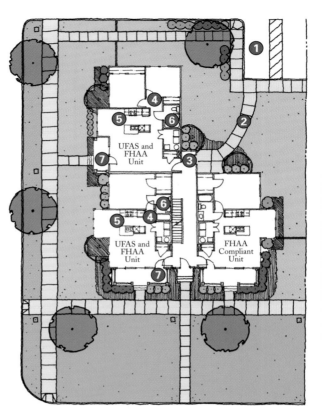

FHAA–Compliant Units

All first-floor units in 4-, 6-, and 8-unit buildings will meet the requirements of the Fair Housing Amendments Act (FHAA).

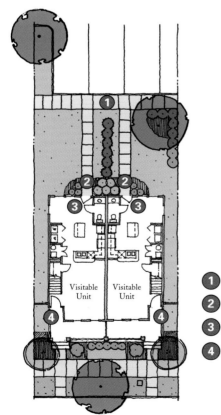

Visitable Townhouse Units

1. Accessible route to building from common area walks and parking
2. Barrier-free entrances
3. 32" clear opening on powder room doors (34" doors)
4. Barrier-free access to porches from units

Visitability will be pursued wherever site conditions and grading permit.

Conceptual Floor Plans and Elevations: Accessibility, Fair Housing Compliance, and Visitability

In the redevelopment, 5% of one-, two-, and three-bedroom units will be UFAS-accessible, all ground-floor apartments will be FHAA-compliant, and as many units as possible will be visitable.

Information current at date of publication.

UDA Writing Style Preferences

Issue	Recommendation
Comma in a series	Use the comma before "and" in a series. For example: Each village is designed to have a village center with shops, restaurants, offices, and apartments.
Feet and inches	In narrative text, spell out feet and inches. In specification text or labeling, symbols are preferred.
Charrette vs. Charette	Charrette (2 r's)
North-South directions	north/south, east/west, northeast, southwest, etc.
Specific vs. generic references	Words like Downtown, City, Master Plan, Preferred Urban Design Plan, X-Ray, and Riverfront have initial capitals only if they refer to a specific reference. For example: Cincinnati's Riverfront Park vs. we propose a riverfront park.
Home owner vs. homeowner	Home owner is two words. Parallels business owner, property owner, etc. However, Homeownership Zone is one word for a specific reference.
Setback vs. set-back	Setback is one word (unless something is set back x feet from the street).

Use of modifiers	Often, words are unnecessarily hyphenated, or hyphenated inconsistently. When used as modifiers, they are hyphenated. For example: mixed income is not hyphenated unless used as a modifier, i.e., mixed-income neighborhood.
	on street (no hyphen) unless on-street parking.
	single family (no hyphen) unless single-family housing.
	Inner city (no hyphen) unless inner-city neighborhood.
Interstate, Route	Always use initial capital letter when used as specific.
Interstate 79 and I-79	When Interstate is spelled out, there is no hyphen between Interstate and number. If abbreviated, e.g., I-79, use the hyphen.
Caption use of periods	If caption forms a complete sentence, use a period. If not, do not use a period.
Acknowledgements vs. Acknowledgments	Although both are correct, for consistency, use the spelling without the "e" following the "g."
Facade vs. Façade	Both are correct, the Americanized version is preferable.
Which vs. that	When to use *which* or *that*:
	Which usually requires a comma, and begins a phrase that is not necessary to the meaning of the sentence. If you can drop the clause and not affect the meaning of the sentence, then *which* is correct.
	That is usually not preceded by a comma and begins a phrase that is crucial to the meaning of the sentence. If you can't drop the phrase, then use *that*.
	For example: John's bulldog, *which* had one white ear, won best in show. The dog *that* won best in show was John's bulldog.

G

How to Draw a UDA Illustrative Plan

Complete each step for
the entire plan, not on a
block-by-block basis.

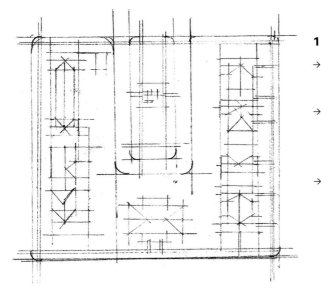

1   Establish Block Guidelines

→   Using a parallel glider, lightly sketch guidelines
    for the block, buildings, sidewalks, and roof lines.

→   Use a circle template at corners and intersections
    (scale will vary depending upon the type of
    block and scale of drawing—"eye it in").

→   Move quickly; don't get hung up on technical
    details.

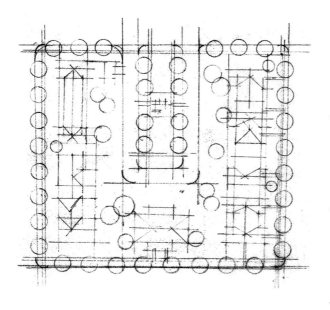

2 Establish Tree Guidelines

→ Trees are an important graphic component in an illustrative plan as they help to convey urban form. They should be drawn with great care.

→ The scale of trees may vary depending upon the urban form that needs to be emphasized, i.e., a boulevard may have larger trees than a typical neighborhood street.

→ Using a circle template, lay out the trees in an orderly fashion. Trees should be drawn slightly larger than true scale and spaced about 25'–30' apart. (Don't measure spacing—just "eye it.")

→ Vary the size of the trees in the front and back yards in a random pattern.
Do this step even if you're rushed!

3 Outline Trees

 Detail

→ After all of the guidelines are established, use a new fine-line, felt-tip pen and lightly draw in the trees—mind your line weights!

→ Trees should be drawn with some detail— not just as circles (see detail).

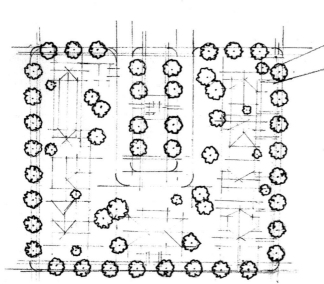

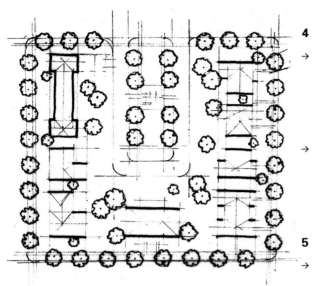

4 Outline Buildings

→ Always rotate the drawing so that your drawing hand is at its most comfortable position for drawing. Draw horizontally from left to right— *not vertically.*

→ Use a marker pen for all new structures; however, garages should be drawn with a fine-line, felt-tip pen.

5 Add Roof Lines (below)

→ Carefully render roof lines using a fine-line, felt-tip pen; rotate drawing as outlined above.

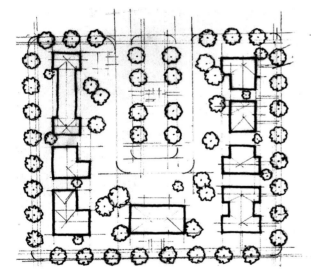

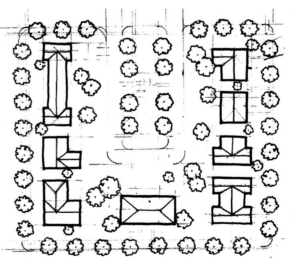

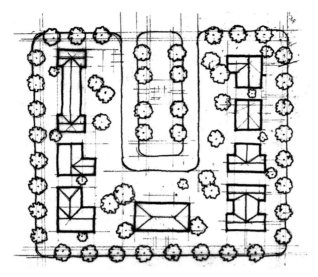

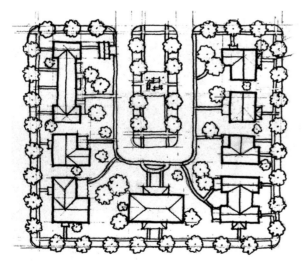

6 Outline Blocks

→ Using a new fine-line, felt-tip pen (you should use fresh pens often), outline the block. Do not draw through trees.

7 Draw Sidewalks and Paths

→ Delicately draw sidewalks (the tip of the pen should barely touch the trace).

→ Do not draw sidewalks through trees, as mentioned above.

8 Clean-up and Final Touches (below)

→ Erase guidelines (a kneaded eraser works best). *Note:* Marker pens will smear on trace if the ink isn't fully dried. Allow the drawing to dry for five minutes or blot with a tissue.

→ Use opaque white correction fluid to correct any mistakes.

→ Stipple grassy areas lightly.

→ Add additional trees and paths to taste. Bake for 45 minutes or until fabulous.

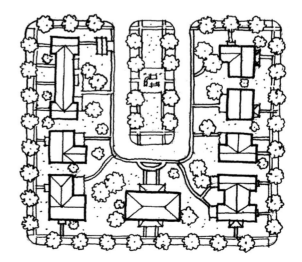

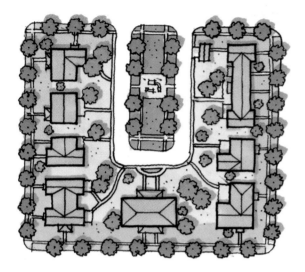

SHADOWS

9   Rendering the Plan

→   In this example from Fort Lewis, Washington, the street and park trees are rendered with dark green.

→   Back yard trees are rendered in bright green.

→   Ornamental flowering trees are rendered with lavender with a dab of purple.

→   Front yard grass is pale blue green.

→   Back yard grass is pale yellow green.

→   The play area/park grass is medium green.

→   All sidewalks and patios are pale yellow.

→   In this example, the houses are new multi-family and are rendered with dark yellow.

→   *Note:*

Shadows

All tree shadows are rendered with medium grey. The shadow is at "2 o'clock" if the drawing is facing north.

→   Building shadows are rendered at the "top" and "right side" of the building if the drawing is facing north. Use a thin shadow for buildings; don't worry about realism—it's about readability.

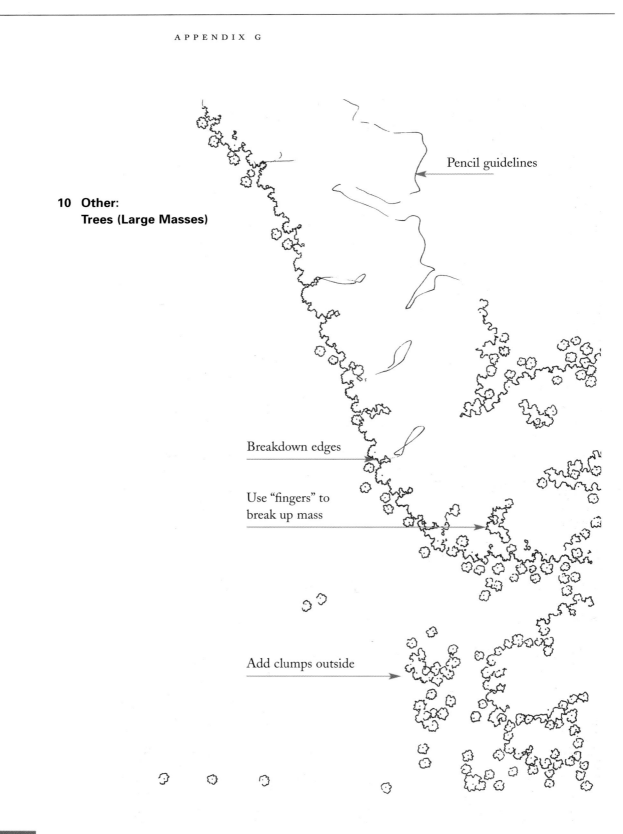

10 Other:
Trees (Large Masses)

Pencil guidelines

Breakdown edges

Use "fingers" to
break up mass

Add clumps outside

INDEX

A

accessibility, 194–96
advisory committee, 54
aerial views, 40, 41
    existing conditions, 89
American Institute of Architects, 10
ARRIS 2001, 185–87
AutoCAD, 186

B

base maps, 64, 93
    city-wide, 70
    immediate area, 72
    impact area, 71
    pattern book development, 148
    preparation, 66, 67–68
    regional, 69
Baxter, South Carolina, 151
blocks and lots
    aerial view, 40
    drawing, 199
    frameworks and development
        patterns, 32
    size, 39
    types, 39
    in urban assembly kit, 33–34
    urban assembly process, 38, 39, 40, 42

building design
    esquisse, 163
    frameworks and development
        patterns, 32
    modernism and tradition, 152
    pattern book analysis, 137–43,
        145–48, 153–54
    pattern book tradition, 131–32
    principles of urban design, 22
    style selection, 40
    urban design and, 9–10, 154
    in urban design process, 13, 33–34,
        39, 40
    use of local style, 106, 155
    see also building design

C

CADD software, 185–87
charrettes, 54
    documentation, 108, 109
    in-house, 95–97, 112–13
    on-site, 95–103, 108, 113–14
    participants, 95
    in pattern book development, 148–49
    purpose, 95
Cincinnati, Ohio, 24–26
client, 51
commercial areas, 38
community, 10, 132
    principles of design, 19
computer technology, 178
    CADD software, 185–87
Congress for the New Urbanism, 18, 19
consultants, 111, 112–13, 156–57

contextual history, 10
copyright protection, 160, 172
corridor design
    frameworks and development
        patterns, 30
    principles of, 21
cross sections, 37

D

data collection, 61, 62–63
    analysis of existing conditions, 66–74,
        158–59
    during first trip, 63–66, 160–61
designers, 51
design process, 12
    advisory committee in, 54
    analysis of existing conditions, 66–68,
        88–93, 98
    charrettes, 54, 95–103, 108, 112–14
    data gathering, 63–64, 160–61
    design team structure and functioning,
        49, 50–51, 156–57
    developing collaboration in, 45–46, 50
    developing vision in, 46
    document maintenance, 108, 109,
        180–92
    drawing techniques and scales,
        164–69, 171–73
    duration, 55
    encouraging participation in, 53
    evolution of design, 104–7, 169–70
    final design documents, 116–25,
        126–29, 172–77